FRAGRANCE OF GOD'S LOVE

By
Marcia Beverly Armstead

TEACH Services, Inc.
www.TEACHServices.com

Copyright © 2010 Marcia Beverly Armstead and TEACH Services, Inc.
ISBN-13: 978-1-57258-609-3
Library of Congress Control Number: 2010935239

Write to:
The Complete Woman/Man Seminars
P.O. Box 17360
Colorado Springs, CO 80935-7360
marcia@completeseminars.org
www.completeseminars.org

Published by

TEACH Services, Inc.
www.TEACHServices.com

DEDICATION

This book is dedicated to my sister Clover Fleming whom God has used to bless and sustain me through the difficult days of my life. Clover does not have a chapter in this book because her kindness to me over the years cannot be contained in a volume.

This work is also dedicated to my son Eugene Jr. who has dedicated more time, effort, and skill to our ministry than anyone I know. He too does not have a chapter in this book, but I am waiting to read his manuscript some day, because he truly has a story to tell.

To my three grandchildren: Eugene III, Elleanna, and Lynnesse whom I love so very, very much.

To my daughters-in-law: Kisha and Suzanne. Thank you for my beautiful grandchildren.

And, to my nieces, nephews, godchildren, and former Vacation Bible School Students scattered throughout the United States, England, Canada, Jamaica, and the Virgin Islands.

CONTENTS

To Brittanni
My dear Coworker
Friend

INTRODUCTION

In the *Fragrance of God's Love* memoirs, Marcia Beverly Armstead draws readers into the very core of her life through the love of her friends. In this book, one becomes familiar not only with the protagonist, but with an entourage of strangers, associates, friends, and family who have made significant contributions to her life.

The chapters encompass her early childhood on the Island of Jamaica, her marriage, the death of her husband, the challenges of widowhood, her remarriage and divorce, her three years of famine and grandeur in Colorado Springs, and the formation and development of her ministries.

Through every phase of her journey there is evidence of a God who has chastened, guided, and sustained her. Marcia's passage portrays an imperfect life, made whole by the blood of the Lamb, and redirected into effective servant leadership.

Her work as president and CEO of The Complete Woman / Man Seminars, as a hospital chaplain, as a radio and television host, and as an ordained elder in her church are by-products of a life once marred and now unblemished because she surrendered her entire life to God.

This book confirms that God does not have favorites and that He still saves men and women, boys and girls, from a life of sin to a life of honor for our good and His glory.

Chapter 1

MY MOTHER

I was fortunate to have been born to a mother who was a Christian. As the third of four children, I was the most spoiled child—perhaps because I looked so much like my father who Mother apparently loved very deeply.

We were born and reared on the Island of Jamaica—Keith, Norma, Clover, and I. We were very close, even though my brother was sixteen years older than Norma and eighteen years older than I. The girls were stair steppers, born when my mother Iris was between the age of thirty-six and forty.

Our mother was one of the town's seamstresses and the organist for our church. She brought us up in the Seventh-day Adventist (SDA) Church where my sisters and I enjoyed learning about the love of God. I believe I speak for all my siblings by saying that the religious foundation given to us in childhood is the greatest gift our mother could have ever bestowed upon us. The knowledge of God and His love is the impetus for our integrity and valued self-esteem. We have never left the church, except in death. Our sister, Norma, passed away in June 1999, and she was faithful to God until the end.

We grew up in a single-parent home. There were advantages and disadvantages with only one parent in the home. The greatest blessing for us was that my siblings and I never heard an argument or witnessed a fight between our parents. We never knew what a domestic dispute was all about, and we thanked God for that. However, we did not have a lot of material things since our father was not at home, and he seldom sent any money to help my mom with our upbringing. Her struggle to be a good parent was observed by neighbors and friends.

When neighbors asked her if they could take us to live with them, just to give her a break, she refused to give us up. She never wanted to see us separated; so neighbors were compelled to leave us alone. After all, we were not that poor!

On the farm, we were somewhat self-sufficient. There were times when we only ate one cooked meal per day, but we never starved because we had at least thirteen fruit trees on our three-acre property. We ate fruit that fell from the trees or that was picked by my older sister, the tomboy who would climb the trees. We had mangoes, apples, bananas, and other fruit. In addition, we ate plenty of coconuts and drank a lot of coconut water. We would help Mother plant and harvest vegetables, and we would kill chickens we owned for meals at special occasions. We never had to purchase eggs or milk because we also had several cows.

Our brother was an adult then, and weekly, he gave Mother a portion of his income so that she could buy flour, sugar, butter, rice, and oil from the store. (Sometimes we made our own butter and our own oil.) We definitely made our own preserves! On occasion, Mother would also have enough money to purchase raw material from the store so she could make our church dresses. We did not have to worry about school clothes because we wore uniforms to school. Life was good from the perspective of a child.

My mother was diagnosed with Type One Diabetes and with hypertension. She died from complications associated with her diseases. However, I knew that she also died from a broken heart. During our growing-up years, Mother would constantly look at pictures of our dad and talk to us about how handsome he was and how much she loved him. Our dad left the island before my youngest sister, Clover, was born. (He had gone to the United States; "skipped" the work contract; and was now living in anonymity.) Our mom went to bed many nights crying because she missed him so much. When I witnessed her undying love for our dad in his absenteeism, I vowed as a child that I would never languish over the lack of love from any man. I would not be like my mom in this respect.

One intentional and wonderful thing Mother did for me was to support my interest in word processing (keyboarding). As a little girl, whenever we went into town, I would always find myself up against the glass window of an office building observing office secretaries typing on the keyboard. It was the most fascinating occupation to me. My mother saw my interest, and one day she bought me a book of poetry and taught me how to read and memorize poetry. The very first poem I learned was "Somebody's Mother" by Mary Dow Brine. My love for poetry allowed me, though very shy as a child, to stand in front of our church congregation with my first recitation. After I was done reciting, there were so many resounding "amen's" that it made me never want to stop my fascination with similar literary works. I not only recited other people's writings, but over the years, I have written several poems of my own.

Mother died when my sisters and I were pre-teenagers. That she died when we were so young was regretful. We could not understand, as children, why God allowed her to be taken from us. The only comfort we had after her death was our love for her life and our love for each other. It was in later years that I was able to thank God for my mother's death, because in her dying, we had the wonderful privilege of migrating to the United States of America—a place where there was no limit to our accomplishments except those we placed on ourselves. Upon our arrival in New York City, we met our dad, but we never lived with him. He died when I was 31 years old.

In the United States, we lived the rest of our childhood years in New York City with an aunt and uncle, Wilhel and Burnett Dixon (who are now both deceased), and with their daughter, Hermine. Our cousin, Hermine, and we grew up together as teenagers and have been very close over the years. Our aunt and uncle were avid worshipers. So, we continued in the spiritual vein in which my mother had fostered.

Through the love of my mother, we were taught to obey the commandments of God and allow Him to reign supreme in our lives. This gave us a value and a merit system that will forever be possessed.

Chapter 2

MY HEROES

Aside from my mother, there are several individuals whom I have admired in life. I have aspired to be like some and have just been inspired by others. Some of these heroes, I have met, and others I have only been familiar with through the medium of television, but they have all been a part of my source of influence.

For many, many years, I was afraid to acknowledge publicly how fascinated I was with singer **Tina Turner**. I believed that revealing this fact would allow people to think I loved rock 'n roll. I do not! When I was a child, growing up in New York City, my siblings and I were forbidden to watch rock 'n roll on television. However, when our aunt and uncle were away from home, I would look through the TV Guide to see if there was a television show where Ike and Tina Turner would be performing, and then I would watch that program. I loved Tina's legs, because I have always had "skinny" legs and could not stand it. Both my sisters were blessed with sizeable legs and great hips, and I felt cheated. Whenever I would see Tina on television, I would focus on her legs and wish that I had inherited big legs.

The closest I came to having legs like Tina was the day I stepped out of my car at a friend's home in Florida and stood for some time in an ant bed—unbeknown to me, of course. I ended up running into her house and going straight to her bathtub to wash the ants off my skin. For the next two weeks, by legs were so painful it was unreal. The one good thing about this mishap was that my legs were swollen enough to look like Tina's. I was so happy I did not know what to do. But, before long, the swelling went down, and my legs were back to normal. Over the years, I have learned to live with my skinny legs and enjoy the fact that I do have legs. And, I still love Tina.

Barbara Walters, an exceptional journalist, was an inspiration to me. When I was young, I would watch her anchor the news on television, and I desired to one day be a journalist. If that was not a possibility, I wanted, then, to one day write feature stories for Barbara. Neither of these dreams became a reality, but she inspired me to be a good English student. Though I may not have been the best student in English, I became proficient in English grammar. Following the professional life of Barbara Walters made me aspire to excel in writing well and speaking well.

Another inspiration was the late **Barbara Jordan** (1936-1996). I admired her not only because she was the first African-American woman to serve in the United States Congress from the South but because she had a command of the English language. I loved to hear her speak and articulate. Whenever she appeared on television, I would be right there watching, not only taking in her words as she spoke out against the unfair treatment of blacks and whites in America, but as she demonstrated that anyone (and certainly any female) can make a profound difference in the world through education. As a child, I aspired to one day speak like Barbara Jordan, not necessarily in tone or content, but in a way that I would be distinctly understood.

It seems quite coincidental now that there is a third Barbara among the list of those I admire: **Barbara Swaby**. I became acquainted with Dr. Swaby when I first arrived in Colorado Springs via educational television. One evening, while flipping channels, I observed her teaching a reading class for the University of Colorado in Colorado Springs. I was attracted to her accent, and believed she had to be a Jamaican (or a JaMerican, as one of my friends calls us). Aside from her enunciation, I was totally captivated by her knowledge of the subject matter and her teaching style. She was (and is) the epitome of professional grace and sophistication. I vowed then that I had to meet this woman. And I prayed, "Lord, please make it possible for us to meet." One day, while in the neighborhood grocery store, I found myself standing in line with Dr. Swaby. This was a God-intended and personable meeting that has been a blessing to me (and hopefully to her). Barbara and I have developed a very wonderful friendship, and we have a mutual admiration for one another and for the work each does.

Another woman who enthralled me during the years her husband was president of the United States is **Hillary Rodham Clinton**. This fascination began when the president took a fall and the world learned of his marital unfaithfulness. I believe that any woman who has had an unfaithful spouse can relate to the hurt and embarrassment that must have resulted for Mrs. Clinton. However, not every woman who has suffered the same heartbreak can relate to the global publicity that this story received. It was during this time, while I prayed for her, that I witnessed an emotionally stalwart woman who braced the incident with everything she could muster to maintain the dignity of the White House, the admiration of the public, and the praise of her family. It must have been hard, but she did it!

I remember one day while in college, we were asked the question, "Who is the one person in the world with whom you would like to spend a three-hour lunch period?" My answer was, "Hillary Rodham Clinton!" My classmates gasped. How sad was their reasoning for what they felt was an unfavorable choice! I believe Mrs. Clinton's experience and response to her private, yet very public challenge, is an excellent example of one spouse who refused to throw in the towel when others may have felt this was the way to go.

Minister Casey Corey has been an inspiration in my adult educational pursuits. I met Casey in 2002 when we were both chaplains at Memorial Hospital in Colorado Springs. We had come into the chaplain's office to complete our visitation reports. After our introductions, and in a very brief conversation, I discovered that Casey had re-entered college in her late fifties and was now a college graduate and an ordained minister. I remember telling her that I was in my early fifties and had not yet finished college; that I had thought about it, but felt it was too late to continue what I had started many years ago. Then Casey said, "It is never too late!" I was so inspired by her jubilance that I re-enrolled in school the next week. I thank Casey for encouraging me to finish college, even though she did not know until five years later that I had enrolled at Colorado Christian University as a result of her influence.

Actually, her encouragement was the final straw to all the prodding I had received from some friends and our consultants over the years. One friend in particular, **Percy Jackson**, when I told him I was thinking about going back to school part time and probably would not finish until age sixty, said, "Marcia, you are going to be sixty anyway. You just need to decide whether you will be sixty with a degree, or sixty without one." Every comment I had ever received about returning to school made sense, but Casey's joy of having accomplished this feat in her later years truly inspired me.

Through the love for my heroes, I realized that I too can be an inspiration to others. God has allowed all these, and numerous other individuals, into my life to motivate and mentor me into the person He wants me to be. I thank Him for my heroes!

Chapter 3

MY HUSBAND

I was married for twenty-three years to my high school sweetheart. I met Eugene Armstead at the Ephesus SDA Church in New York City. He was in the youth choir, and I was an usher. We attended separate high schools. He went to an all-boys' school in Manhattan; and I attended an all-girls' school in the Bronx.

We started dating (going out socially) at age sixteen with the permission of my uncle, who was very strict. Gene had an identical twin brother, Ernest, and an older brother Joseph Jr. Ernest's girlfriend's name was Gwendolyn Wilson, and Joe's fiancée was Geraldine Armstrong. We all became friends and did a lot of things together. When Joe and Gerri were married, we spent a lot of time over at their home. We have all remained close over the years.

At age eighteen, after Gene and I graduated high school, he was drafted into the United States Army. Gene was a medical specialist in the army and a conscientious objector. During his tour of duty in Vietnam, he earned a Good Conduct Medal, an Army Commendation Medal, a National Defense Service Medal, a Vietnam Service Medal, two Purple Hearts, and a Bronze Star. When his overseas deployment ended and he returned home, we were married while he was still in the service of his country.

After an honorable discharge from the U.S. Army, Gene decided to attend college. Since he was a medic in the military, he wanted to be a doctor and to commence his pre-med studies at Oakwood College, now Oakwood University. He told me that no one in his immediate family had ever graduated from college, and he wanted to be the first.

Since he knew I was not ready to leave my family in New York, Gene spent one year attending college in New

9

York City so I could adjust to the thought of leaving. It was painful for me to leave New York. I was leaving my sisters; my brother; my boss, "Mr. Roslind" at RKO Radio; and all my friends, who I had treasured for the twelve years I lived in that city. Well, the time came when we knew we could not delay any longer. Time was fleeting and Gene had a goal in mind.

My boss was very sad. He offered to pay Gene's college tuition to any university in New York if this would have allowed me to continue working for him, but his offer was futile. Mr. Roslind and I had a very special bond. You see, he was not the easiest boss. When I was first hired to work for him, I was told by others who knew my boss that this employment would not last any longer than three months, because all the previous administrative assistants had quit because of his abrasive personality. Well, I was hired to be his assistant, and I was determined that my professional as well as human-relations skills would keep me employed there. I worked for Mr. Roslind for almost three years and that employment terminated only because of Gene's quest to attend Oakwood College.

While working for RKO Radio, I had the privilege of meeting and seeing many television stars and radio personalities. I was able to watch a studio performance by The Supremes, and I met two of my favorite actors in an elevator: Peter Falk of *Columbo* and Ben Gazzara of *Run for Your Life* who had come to promote their 1970 movie, *Husbands*. It was a brief conversational exchange, but a wonderful experience for me. I also met Geoffrey Holder in passing, also in the elevator. It was exciting to work at a place where promotional work was done for the stars.

Now, it was time to depart for Huntsville, Alabama. I must say that Oakwood College was the best thing that ever happened to me. The best four years of my life were spent at the Oakwood campus and living in Huntsville. Two years after attending Oakwood College, and three and half years after we were married, our son, Eugene Jr., was born. I remember praying not to have any children, but if we did, "Dear

God, please make them boys!" It was wonderful to have a male child, and I was glad God answered my prayer.

One year after attending Oakwood, Gene came to me and said he was changing his curriculum. Now, he wanted to be a pastor instead of a doctor. That was the saddest news I could have ever heard. I did not want to be a pastor's wife. However, I hid my disappointment and pretended to be very excited about his decision. That day began a silent, inward rebellion against God for putting me in such a predicament. I determined then that whatever a theology student's wife was supposed to be, I was going to be the opposite; whatever a pastor's wife was required to do, I would behave in an adverse manner. Sadly, I upheld this commitment through most of our married life.

Sure, I was a supportive student's wife. I worked in the administrative offices of the college for four and a half years, assisting in every way possible to help my husband through school. When he became a pastor, I was very dutiful—a wonderful hostess both at the church and at home, and I always represented well the "first-lady" status that was required by his congregants, but inside, the inward silent rebellion continued.

During our last year at Oakwood College, when conference presidents came down to look over the "crop" of senior theology students soon to graduate and seeking placement, we were present for the announcements of those who had been recruited to pastor churches within the different conferences. My husband was not one of the blessed few hired to work as a pastor, and we were very disappointed. However, Gene did not verse or show his disappointment outwardly, but I certainly did.

On one memorable Sabbath afternoon, at the end of the Allegheny West Conference recruitment day at the school, there was a scheduled meeting in Moran Hall. Since Gene loved taking pictures and was the campus photographer, we were always first at almost all the events on campus. As Gene, "little Gene," and I entered the building, the auditorium was overrun with foot-washing basins still containing water—that morning there had been a foot-washing/communion service in the auditorium, and no one had cleaned up.

My husband exclaimed, "Just look at this place!" And I said, "Yep! It's a mess. I guess the conference president and his new hires need to come and clean it up."

President Harold Cleveland of the Allegheny West Conference then came into the room. He folded his hands and shook his head. Gene immediately handed me our baby and rushed over to Elder Cleveland. He said, "Doc, we can clean this up in no time. Put your papers down and let's get started." Needless to say, I was furious! As I sat and watched my husband and the conference president picking up basins and dumping water, I was still rebelling. However, in approximately fifteen minutes, the auditorium was clean and ready for the jubilant program that was planned for the new pastors and their families. Even though I was still fuming, I realized that my husband was truly a man of honor.

With no offer of an internship with any of the regional conferences, after graduation, Gene accepted a fellowship to Howard University in Washington, DC. I was employed as an administrative assistant to two vice presidents at the General Conference of Seventh-Day Adventists, North American Division (GC/NAD). It was a position I should never have held because the newspaper ad that ran for this job stated that they were looking for an administrative assistant who was tri-lingual, speaking English, Spanish, and French, and knowledgeable of sign language to work with the hearing impaired constituency. The only languages I spoke were Jamaican *patois*, English, and *Ebonics*, and I had absolutely no knowledge of sign language! I applied anyway because I knew my word processing and administrative skills (typing, shorthand, Dictaphone transcription, and letter composition) would blow them out of the water. It did. And I was employed at the most magnificent place that I have ever worked.

One of the administrators there was Elder E.E. Cleveland. One day he stopped by my office to talk. When he learned who I was and that I was married to Eugene Armstead Sr., he said, "My brother, Harold, has been looking for that guy. Tell your husband to give Harold a call. Here is his number." I had only been at the GC for six months and was praying this was not going to be another residential move for us. I was tempted not to pass the message on but knew I had to. My husband contacted Harold Cleveland, and we were invited to his home. While there the president offered my husband an internship within the Allegheny West conference. It was at his dining table that he reminded us of something Gene and I had both forgotten. He took us back to Moran Hall at Oakwood College and stated that after that experience, he came back home wondering how he could include such "a man of honor" on his team. This is how my husband entered the gospel ministry.

We had to move again! I was tearful, leaving my employment at the GC, but I realized that even though our tenure there was short, we came away with some beautiful memories.

I remember, and thank, the HR Department at the GC for refusing to grant me permanent employee status until my diagnosis of Type One Diabetes was under control. Oh, I knew I had this inherent disease. The finding was made at Huntsville Hospital when I was pregnant with our son, but I was in severe denial, left the hospital untreated, and refused to go back for any follow-up exams. To become a permanent employee at the GC, I had to be medicated with insulin twice daily. I could not face the thought of ever injecting myself every day, but I knew it had to be done. The day I was to have gone for medical training on how to do this "hideous" task, I asked Gene to accompany me to the medical center. He said he couldn't because he had a very important exam at Howard University that morning that he could not miss. I was so disappointed.

However, while sitting in the treatment room with the nurse and telling her, "I cannot do this!" I looked up through my tears, and there was Gene walking in. He said, "Bev, it is going to be alright. You must learn how to do it." He then took a needle with placebo and injected himself. Then he said, "This is all you have to do. Now, you do me." I followed his lead and injected him. Then he said, "You can do the same to yourself; try it." I did. Then I looked at him with eyes still filled with tears and smiled. It was then that I realized I did not marry a perfect man, but we had a perfect love.

Gene was an intern in the Allegheny West Conference for approximately two years before entering the seminary. During that time, I worked as administrative assistant to two department heads: Elder Willie J. Lewis and Elder Henry Wright. Shortly before leaving for Andrews University (AU) to work on his Masters of Divinity, we adopted our second son, Shirley Johnson Jr., who we subsequently named, Jonathan Keith Armstead. God had now given us two sons.

Our three and a half years at AU were rough. Not only were the Michigan winters unbearable (especially the blizzard of 1978), but we were "victims" of adoption fraud. We soon discovered that our son, Jon, had some medical problems that were undisclosed by the adoption agency in Ohio. His prognosis was bleak; our son was disabled and would be for the rest of his life. When we learned of Jon's lifelong physical problems, my first instinct was to take him back to the agency, but Gene said, "No. We are in a position to care for him, and if not us, who will be the ideal parents for this little boy?" So, we accepted the challenges and responsibilities of working, going to school, and caring for a special-needs child. Since my husband had always said he wanted nothing from the government, Gene never filed for his eligible disability after the Vietnam War, and we never applied for disability benefits for Jon all the years that my husband was alive. Actually, we did not know what benefits were available, as my husband refused to even look in that direction.

Well, here we were—my husband in graduate school and working two jobs; I was attending college and working at AU as well. However, our son's emotional needs and physical condition demanded more time at home. Some sacrifices had to be made. It was important that Gene finish school so our family could move to a higher socioeconomic level. It was also imperative that I continue to work (if not full time, then part time); however, our son's needs required me to relinquish my higher education pursuit. I quit college and soon after that took personal leave from my job. Our disabled child needed much of our time, and we had another son who needed our attention, love, and care as well.

Jon had numerous surgeries throughout his lifetime, but the four major surgeries of his early childhood were while my husband was in graduate school. I had to leave my husband and older son at AU while spending months in children's hospitals with our youngest. At that time, we had also severed ties with the Allegheny West Conference (or them with us), and we were on our own with providing health insurance and the like without professional sponsorship. But, God saw us through.

The hardest decision for me was quitting college and having to see my peers excel academically while I remained at home. While at home, I edited and typed many term papers and masters' thesis for my peers. I also assisted with my husband's research for his seminary papers. I felt as though I *was* in school but others were getting the credit. When I talked with God about how I felt, He assured me that if I forfeited my ambitious pursuits and willingly cared for our son, He would bless me over and above what I could ever hope or think. And, He did.

When there was some stability to Jon's health, I was able to resume full-time employment. There were times when I was privy to the annual salaries of my former college friends (with degrees), and I learned that my wages with the federal government far exceeded theirs. At times, my income was even greater than my husband's. This is one way God chose to bless me, and this blessing continued for many, many years.

Even with the grinding days in Michigan, there were happy occasions. Some of my more joyous times were spent sitting at the feet of **Pastor Saint Claire Phipps**. I remember days when my husband would look out the window of our home toward the campus and say, "Here comes

Pastor Phipps. Boys, get the stool for your mom!" My family knew that when Pastor Phipps visited, it was learning time—I would always sit at his feet.

I remember one day telling Pastor Phipps, when we were alone, how silently rebellious I was and how I just wanted to do things contrary to the high ideals I knew God had for me in this profession that my husband has chosen. When he asked why I would go out of my way to engage in unbecoming behaviors, I told him that perhaps the things I wanted to do I must have inherited from my family tree. In response to that statement, Pastor Phipps said, "When one is born again, genealogy has no place in that new life." Wow, what a friend! It was at that point that I started to gradually change my attitude and my behaviors.

When Gene graduated from Andrews University, I was able to disclose to him, for the very first time, how I felt about him changing his undergraduate major and going into the pastoral field. I still did not tell him that I was rebelling and that I did not want to be a pastor's wife, but I expressed how disappointed I was that he had changed his major from pre-med to theology. I congratulated him for his achievements and vowed that I would continue to support him in the ministry. What he said to me that day, I will never forget. He said, "Bev, now that I am done with school, and since you have sacrificed so much for us (our family), I want you to go back to college and/or do whatever it is you wish. I thank you so much for seeing me through." Then, he kissed me! I did not go back to school then, but I felt happy that my hard work had been acknowledged by the only person from whom it really mattered.

After AU, we continued to live in Berrien Springs, Michigan, as Gene was not yet hired by another conference to do pastoral work. I prayed that we would once again get "picked up." Six months after graduation, after much prayer and hoping, we received a call from President James Edgecombe of the Southeastern Conference located in Orlando, Florida, inviting Gene to come and be the pastor of the Winter Park, Apopka, and Sanford district. What a happy day that was for us! We were glad to move to a warmer climate and grateful for the "Southern hospitality" we found among the parishioners there.

Being a pastor's wife was not always easy because of the many times we relocated, the many times our sons had to change schools, and the high expectations of many congregants. Though it was a difficult time for me, as I look back, I realize that being the wife of a pastor polished me and ultimately saved me from a life of ruin.

The years we spent in Florida were blissful. I went from working with Adventist Health Systems North in Stevensville, Michigan, to being employed with Adventist Health Systems South in Orlando, Florida. Then, after completing twelve years of service to the church, we moved to Tampa, Florida, where I was hired by the Federal Deposit Insurance Corporation (FDIC). When I interviewed for the job as administrative assistant to the director of the local FDIC office, I left praying that I would not receive a job offer. It was not the smoke-free environment to which I had become accustomed, and I could not bear smelling cigarette smoke. But I was offered the job, and I took it. Because of nationally increased health awareness and local legislation, it was not long before I was able to work in a smoke-free office. I was an FDIC employee for approximately eight of our eleven years in Florida. We loved that state, and our sons spent most of their growing-up years there.

Gene's last pastorate was in Daytona Beach, Florida, where he was assigned by the conference to build a church for that congregation. Instead of building, we were able to purchase a one-million-dollar facility for six hundred thousand dollars. It was a mission fulfilled and a great acquisition for the congregation and the conference. While Gene ministered in Daytona Beach, I still worked for the FDIC, but this time in Orlando. I worked sixty-five miles away from home, so we had a house in Daytona Beach where Gene and our sons maintained permanent residence, and I had a small apartment in Orlando. I usually departed from Daytona Beach early on Monday mornings and journeyed to work in Orlando. I would return home on Tuesday evenings in time for prayer meeting; then back to Orlando again early Wednesday morning, not to return until Friday evening to spend the weekend with my family. In spite of the constant commute, our family maintained low levels of dysfunction and spent a lot of quality time together.

It was during those long-distance travel times that I wrote an article for our shepherdess newsletter titled, "A Commuting Mom Can Survive." This article was basically written for me specifically, as I sought answers to this piece of my life's puzzle. Leaving my children to travel long distances to maintain a high-paying job was heartbreaking at times. I remember once as I drove away from home asking God: "What will become of my children if something happens at school while I am so far away and while their dad is involved with a church engagement and neither of us is close by to attend to the situation?" His answer, *"I am the One who takes care of your children whether you are away from them or right beside them. Just trust in Me!"* After this affirmation, I never again worried about the safety of my children during my absence or my presence.

While residing in Daytona Beach, and still commuting, I developed a case of insomnia, which lasted for approximately eight months. I could not sleep at night, and I was never sleepy in the daytime while driving or while holding down a high tech position as a liquidation technician for the FDIC. During the period of this illness, I felt I was going to die. I prayed to God to heal me, and I had the faith that He would, but I knew it would be a conditional healing—I had to give up my "secret" sin, and I had to finally cease being rebellious. God had showed me clearly that 99.9 percent of my life wouldn't do. He wanted 100 percent of my allegiance. That month, and only then, I fully surrendered my life to God. I told Him that if He would forgive me of my sins and heal me from insomnia, I would serve Him for the rest of my life. After that full surrender and knowing God had forgiven me of my iniquity, the Holy Spirit took charge of my life. I was completely healed within three weeks, and I started, once again, to sleep restfully and peacefully at night.

18

I willingly and anxiously began to read my Bible more; I read inspirational/devotional books (one devotional book in particular written by Ellen G. White: *Our Father Cares*); I changed the repertoire of music I listened to in my car from Country & Western and Classics, to hymns and old-time gospel. I loved the new focus! I had become a brand new woman. The new me had a new taste and a free-will desire to please God in all that I did. He was now beginning to speak to me and through me. I became familiar with His voice; I listened with an intelligent ear, and I was obedient to Him.

One Monday morning in September 1991 while traveling from Daytona Beach to Orlando, about three months after being healed, the Holy Spirit visited me in my car. He said, *"You told God you would serve Him if He healed you. You have been healed. You need to prepare now to serve Him."* Wow! What an attention-getter; what a serious charge!

As I always traveled with a large yellow pad and pencils in my car, I immediately grabbed the utensils I needed to write down my instructions. It was in the car that morning that the ministry of The Complete Woman / Man Seminars was born. The vision, the mission, and the scope of the ministry were laid out before me prior to arriving at my place of employment.

This newly assigned divine task really frightened me. I told God that I only had a high school diploma and less than two years of college, and He said, *"This is how I want you."* Then I reminded Him that I could not speak eloquently enough to do this task and that I was just a writer, and He said, *"This is why I have called you."* I continued to argue that this ministry would need staff and/or volunteers. He said, *"I will do the recruiting for you."* Then I said, "Lord, this work is going to need capital, and I do not have the money for this!" He replied, *"I will supply every need of yours."* Thus, I ended the argumentative discourse and proceeded to just ask God for directions. I am glad that while I was still married, God called me to do a work for Him and my husband gave his full support.

In January 1992, one morning while at my apartment in Orlando getting ready for work, I was in the process of combing my hair in front of the mirror, and I saw a vision. It may have lasted a minute or possibly only thirty seconds, but my conscious mind was gone.

The Vision

In the vision, I stood looking at a large white wall. On the wall were three items of great significance:

1. The date—June 1992
2. A sum of money—$660,000, and
3. A dial on which the pointer moved 180 degrees.

I knew this was symbolic. Without knowing the true meaning of the vision, I assumed that something was going to happen in six months. It had to be something good, since all that money was part of the event, and it indicated that not just mine, but my entire family's lives were going to take a 180-degree turn.

After returning to reality, I had a strong feeling that I could not talk about what I had just witnessed, but I was excited about it and lived the next several months virtually on cloud nine because of this wonderful thing I perceived was going to happen for my family.

As the days, weeks, and months passed, I began to feel that what I thought was good news was really bad news. Over the next several months, as I journeyed back to Daytona Beach from Orlando, I noticed that my husband was losing weight and acquiring some dermatological changes (spots) to his face and legs. I urged him to go to the doctor, but he did not. As we got closer to **June 1992**, it was evident that my husband was very ill. Much against his will, on June 28, 1992, he ended up in the emergency room of our local hospital and was diagnosed with Acute Lymphocytic Leukemia. He refused to be admitted to the hospital and released himself from their care. His reasoning was that he had to finalize plans for an upcoming evangelistic tent effort in the city of Daytona Beach and there was no time to be sick. Against medical advice and my constant urging during the week that followed, he refused to place himself under medical care.

A few days later while at the FDIC, Eugene Jr., who was on his summer break from Forest Lake Academy in Orlando, called and said, "Mom, something is wrong with Daddy. For the past two days, he has had me driving him around to his business appointments, and today he can hardly walk. He is leaning on me a lot, and I am so tired." I told Eugene to drive his dad directly to the emergency room of our local hospital and that I was on my way. Needless to say, now I had a partial interpretation of the meaning to the vision I had six months earlier. Yes! The date was right on; and, Yes! Our lives (my husband's, mine, and our sons' lives) would be forever changed. Yet, I had no idea what the six hundred and sixty thousand dollars meant, but that was not important now.

Upon re-examination, the attending physician gave my husband two weeks to live. However, Gene's life was preserved for six months with radical chemotherapy and radiation treatments in order to prepare his body for a bone marrow transplant. His identical twin brother (same DNA) had consented to participate in a bone marrow transplant. The bone marrow transplant surgery was very successful, but it did not save Gene's life. During the process of his post surgical recuperation, Gene was transfused with tainted blood, and he was further diagnosed with Hepatitis C, which his immune system could not combat. This led to multi-organ failure, thus losing his battle for life on January 11, 1993.

During the six months of Gene's illness, I was afforded the opportunity of personally knowing his mother, **Margaret Armstead**, and what a dear person she was. She left her home in New York City to spend all that time in Daytona Beach and later in Tampa at her son's side (with the exception of two weeks when she returned home to handle some personal business). My mother-in-law watched peaceful, prayerfully, and quietly as her son struggled to live. During that time, she was torn between two sons, as her older son, Joseph Jr., was also hospitalized in California, undergoing a triple by-pass heart surgery, but she never left Gene's side. Her daughter, **Francella Chisholm**, was ever so faithful in keeping the family together. Francella flew back and forth from New York to California and to Florida, keeping tabs on everyone while trying to keep her home fires burning. I don't know what I would have done without such a wonderful sister-in-law. Gene's brother, Joseph, survived but was not told of his brother's death until doctors were sure he was out of the woods.

The love that was displayed toward us from the church members, my husband's colleagues and former classmates, and also my coworkers at FDIC was overwhelming. Their acts of kindness were so numerous that I am unable to chronicle them all, but I will make mention of just a few. One church member from our former church in Tampa, **Fannie Wynn**, hired a limousine service to drive us from the hospital in Daytona Beach to the surgery site in Tampa, Florida. Because my husband was mobile, the hospital denied ambulance service and the family was responsible for transport. I don't know how this dear sister knew I could not be depended on to drive safely, because I was so tired and worn out. But she knew. Fifteen minutes into the limousine ride, my mother-in-law, my husband, and I fell asleep and did not awake until we arrived at our destination. God knew what we needed and He made provisions through the Wynn family.

Our good friends from the Clearwater church, **Betty and Barry Hogan**, came to our home while I was at the hospital and filled all our cabinets with groceries—enough to feed all the family members and friends that were coming in and out of the house on a daily basis. **Daisy and Fred Palmer** from the Winter Park church brought enough groceries into our house one day to cover the floor of our living room. Gene's classmate, **Lloyd Rahming, MD**, and our friend, **Donnette Dwyer-Williams, MD**, spent hours by his bedside and with the family, interpreting all the medical jargon into layman's terms. **Elder Donald Walker** from the Southeastern Conference spent some of the last hours with him singing hymns from the hymnal. Friends we grew up with in New York City, **Annette and Alonzo Wilson**, flew in just for a visit.

My friends and coworkers at the FDIC gave numerous leave hours so that I could be on paid leave from work throughout the length of my husband's illness and for seven weeks after his death. My boss/coworker, **Esther Mateos**, would call me almost every day, and ask, "Marcia, where are you today (psychologically)? What do you need?" Esther and I became such good friends, and she has extended herself time and time again to help our family. She spoke at Gene's funeral and gave the most impressive greeting and acknowledgement I had ever heard.

Rachelle Hayes, a nurse and a good family friend, allowed our younger son, while we were in Tampa, to stay at her home, and she took care of his school attendance and homework. (Jon could not live with us for two months because the doctors were afraid of my husband's exposure to any transferable microbes from school-children's association because of his low immune system.)

In the final two weeks of life, **Daisy and Roy Brown** came to the hospital, and after having worship with the family in the hospital's waiting room, they invited me out to dinner. "Oh, no," I said. "I can't leave Gene now." But, they prevailed by asking, "If you stay, what can you do for him?" It was then that I realized there was nothing more I could do for Gene, and we went to dinner. This was a welcome and most therapeutic break!

Our good friend **Edna Taylor** came to visit during the last week of Gene's life, and as she looked at the grave situation and saw he was not going to make it, she asked, "Marcia, has Pastor Armstead ever filed for disability from the injuries sustained while in the U.S. military?" I told her, "No; of course not!" I reiterated that Gene said as long as he could work and the pins that held his fingers together did not fail him, he would not collect a dime from the United States government. Edna lovingly grabbed my elbow, looked into my eyes, and said, "Come with me. We need to go down to the Veteran Administration (VA) and get an application for you to fill out. He is not gone yet, and others can witness his 'X' on the signature line." She drove me to the VA and back to the hospital, and on my husband's death bed, he applied for disability. If this had not been done, neither my sons nor I could have received benefits after his death. What a wonderful friend! Thank you, Edna.

Two days before Gene died, I placed an urgent telephone call to **Pastor Wesley Bruce**, then pastor of the Mount Calvary SDA Church in Tampa and a former Vietnam buddy of Gene's. When I told his secretary who I was, she stated that the pastor was in a meeting, but if I would standby, she would interrupt. When Pastor Bruce came to the telephone, I told him that Gene did not have long and asked him if he could come. Pastor Bruce said he would wrap up the meeting and would come directly to the hospital. As my mother-in-law and I waited for him to arrive, we looked up and saw his wife, **Jenett Bruce**, exiting the elevator. When I asked the pastor's wife what she was doing there, she stated that her husband had called her and indicated that he would be delayed, so she left her office and came right over. She then patted my arm and said, "Everything is going to be alright." Then, she went into the room where my husband laid and prayed over him until Pastor Bruce arrived.

This gesture by Sister Bruce did more for me and my mother-in-law than I can ever explain. Months and years later, my mother-in-law had wonderful memories of all the kind gestures she witnessed, and while she had forgotten a lot of the names of people who came and went, she never forgot Jenett Bruce. This also made a profound impression on me. I learned that day the efficacy of a compassionate and truly dutiful pastor's wife, and it made me understand the true role that such a title demands. If Pastor Bruce had never arrived, the fact that his wife reported in would have been enough for me.

In Gene's dying, many things we took for granted while he lived, were confirmed. First and foremost, I learned that being a pastor was not just a job for him. He truly loved his members, and they loved him. I also realized that nothing, and no one, can take the place of a father with his sons, and I knew beyond the shadow of a doubt that my husband sincerely loved me. One day as we walked the corridors of the Oncology Unit in the hospital, he said, "Bev, I am glad this happened to me and not to you." What love!

The last six months of my husband's life were the saddest, yet the happiest time we ever spent together. Here was a man whom we shared with hundreds of congregants every week, but for the first time in his professional life, it seemed his family had become his main focus. We experienced a bond that we had never shared before, and we endured a separation that we could not have ever imagined.

I wanted my husband to live, but it was now evident that the vision I had in January 1992 was about his death. The day before my husband died, I went into the bathroom of his hospital room, locked the door; and on my hands and knees, clawed the floor like a wounded animal. I begged the Lord to let him live, but God told me he was going to die and that I needed to go into the room and say good-bye. As I dried my tears and cleaned myself up, I went to the bed where my husband laid (in a comatose state) and said good-bye to him. I told him that I would be fine and that his sons would be taken care of. This was probably the hardest thing I had ever done in my life.

A few hours later as I sat by the door of his hospital room, I saw my best girlfriend, B. Jean Anderson, walking down the hallway to visit. She and her family had traveled from Orlando to Tampa. Jean had a book in her hand. When she handed me the book, she said, "Bev, I didn't know what to bring you. I know there is nothing I can do for Gene, but there is certainly something I can do for you. God asked me to bring you this little book as there is something He wants you to know." I opened the book and my eyes focused on a quote from Psalm 46:10: "Be still and know that I am God..." That was exactly what I needed, and God settled me at that very moment to accept what He was about to do.

At Gene's funeral, classmates, family, friends, and other pastors came from out of state. We were especially thrilled to see **Evangelist Walter Pearson** and **Pastor Lawrence Hamilton** who drove all through the night from Atlanta, Georgia, to Tampa, Florida, not to participate, but just to attend the ceremonies. Gene's step-mother, **Wilhelmina Armstead**; his brother Jonathan; sister-in-law, Johnnie; and sister, Lorraine, drove down from Washington, DC. **Pastor Robert Conner**, who married us on December 14, 1969, flew from New York City to do one of the most appropriate eulogies I had ever heard. Of course, Gene had been in communication with him from his hospital bed and had requested to be eulogized by Pastor Conner.

Not too long after Gene's death, I left Orlando for Atlanta, Georgia. Traveling to Atlanta with our good friend **Marvin Blackmon**, who drove the U-Haul truck for me, I told him about the vision I had had and how even now, a year later, I still did not know the meaning of the six hundred and sixty thousand dollars. Marvin said, "I can help you with part of the interpretation." Then he asked, "What was the cost of the church building in Daytona Beach that your husband's congregation purchased?" I answered, "Six hundred thousand dollars." Then Marvin said, "Now, you figure out the rest." As I traveled in the cab of that truck with Marvin, I calculated every financial contract in which both Gene and I had been liable or from which we both benefited: the small equity in our house; the insurance reimbursement on his automobile; the amount the IRS forgave; our indebtedness on a bank loan; the cost of his funeral; the life insurance benefit from the conference received after his death; and the amount that was contributed to his Leukemia Fund. The sum total was exactly sixty thousand dollars. When I put my pad and pencil down, the Holy Spirit said to me, *"Now you begin the first day of the rest of your life."*

Through the love of my husband, I was able to pursue my dreams and be the woman I chose to become. He depended on me heavily as a wife, a mother, and a friend. Yet he never interfered with or impeded my progress. And, even though I never wanted to be a pastor's wife, I honored the position God had allowed me to fill, and I became thankful to Him for having placed me in this lifestyle. The experience made me a better person, allowed my children a degree of well-roundedness, and drew my husband and me closer together—and to God.

Fragrance of God's Love

Chapter 4

COLLEGE FRIENDS

Perhaps no other friendships are as long lasting as the friendships that are congealed during the course of campus life. At Oakwood College, Gene and I were blessed to have developed interpersonal relationships with international students, and from these relationships, we solidified mutual attraction and appreciation.

Our first campus friend was actually someone we had known for many years. We had arrived at Oakwood two months after she had; she was not a student, but the secretary for then President C. B. Rock. **Darleen Williams** had been attending the same church in New York City that we had been attending. When Gene and I arrived on campus, we were disappointed to learn that the on-campus housing we had applied for was not ready for occupancy. As we sat on the fender of the U-Haul truck, in which we had just driven from New York to Alabama, tired, sweaty, and disgusted, it seemed that Darleen appeared out of nowhere. She looked down from the balcony of the Blake Center building and called, "Hey, Gene! Hey Bev! What's going on? Come on up!" When we entered Darleen's office and told her of our dilemma, she made a few phone calls, and within two hours, we moved into an on-campus apartment where we lived for a year prior to purchasing our very first home, which was off campus. Throughout our four and a half years at Oakwood, Darleen and I were almost inseparable.

Not long after arriving on campus, I was employed by the Office of Development and Public Relations for the college, so since we both worked for the administration, we spent a lot of our lunch periods together. Darleen, Gene, and I were chaperones for our campus "children"—*The Dynamic Five*—Donny Barnes, Gary Wimbish, Van Runnels, Michael Smith, and Craig Dossman (a male singing group) who traveled almost every weekend to share their musical talents with other organizations.

Darleen and I were together whenever possible. I drove with Darleen on my very first trip to Florida, and when we had our first son, Darleen became one of his Godmothers. Darleen, Gene, and I spent almost every Thanksgiving holiday together during college. Even after Gene graduated and we moved away, we drove from Berrien Springs, Michigan, to Huntsville, Alabama, so I could stand as the matron of honor at Darleen's wedding, when she married **Horace "Mike" Simmonds**. When both our families left Oakwood and Darleen moved back to New York after her marriage, she and Mike would still travel to wherever we were residing so we could spend Thanksgiving together.

Darleen, a professional singer, sang at my husband's ordination in Hawthorne, Florida, and she also sang in Tampa, Florida, at his funeral service. When I was widowed and remarried, at Darleen's invitation, I had the awesome privilege of returning to the Ephesus Church in Harlem, New York, as guest speaker and seminar presenter for a Women's Day program.

There are so many unmentioned, and unmentionable, stories that have been a part of our experiences on, and away from, the Oakwood campus. These experiences are all woven into a pattern of unconditional friendship.

Dianne and Alfred Hampton are two other friends with whom we became acquainted while at Oakwood College. During the first year that we lived in the married students' apartments on campus, they were our neighbors. We would always remind each other how thin the walls were, and when Dianne became pregnant with their first son, Alfred Jr., the joke was that this was a *contagious* condition. A myth! But, believe it or not, three months later, I became pregnant as well. Dianne and Alfred had two boys and so did we.

Years after Gene graduated from college and the seminary and we moved to Orlando, Florida, we met Dianne and the boys again, and our friendship continued to blossom.

Our boys and the Hampton boys engaged in a lot of the same sports, church, and school activities. Now that our children are adults and Dianne and I are both single women, she and I occasionally team up for vacations and especially alumni weekend visits at Oakwood. Our bond of friendship will never be broken.

Linda and Wintley Phipps are also two very dear friends who have meant a lot to us. Gene and I used to travel with Wintley, and Wintley would travel with us as we reached out from the campus to visit dark counties—preaching, singing, and evangelizing while at Oakwood. We loved to hear Wintley's beautiful baritone. We always knew he would excel musically, and he has.

Wintley's wife Linda, the Floridian, was the sweetest young lady you ever wanted to meet. She adored Wintley, and he adored her. Even today they remain very much in love and are very humble individuals. I will never forget how encouraging Linda was to me as we talked one day about my youngest son's disabilities. She was able to share with me how God had sustained her extended family as they experienced a similar situation with a family member. She talked faith and hope into my heart, and I was blessed.

When Wintley hosted his first television show in Washington, DC, he invited Gene to be his guest. My husband was honored and excited to be able to talk about some of his experiences while serving in Vietnam. Wintley and Linda were gracious hosts, and Gene truly enjoyed his weekend with them. Notwithstanding Wintley's singing engagements that took him all over the world, he always took the time to support former classmates. Consequently, he came to our Winter Park and Tampa/Clearwater districts, where he blessed our congregations and community with his musical talents.

While living in Colorado Springs, I have had the privilege of spending some fun time with the Phipps whenever they visit this city. I love it when Linda accompanies Wintley on these trips, for then I know that I will be invited to have dinner with them or just sit and chat in their hotel suite. When

Wintley travels without Linda, I am only able to be an audience participant at his performances. He is a man of exceptional fidelity and a wonderful friend.

Many of our college friends have been transitory, but all my friendships are eternal, faithful, and encouraging. Some of my campus friends may not have a chapter in this book, but there are many who have initiated significant changes in my life and deserve honorable mention. One of these is **Harold L. Lee** who was the director of development, and my boss, while I worked at Oakwood. Under his professional administrative tutelage, I became proficient in letter composition. He was the first, and only, administrator from whom I have learned numerous administrative skills and public relations techniques. To him, I am forever grateful!

Mary and Malcolm Taylor were married students at Oakwood when we were enrolled. Malcolm and Gene were classmates, and Mary, as I, was a supporting wife. When I left employment as administrative assistant for development at Oakwood, Mary was my successor. Years later when I left my position at Adventist Health Systems, Sunbelt in Orlando, Mary was my successor in that position as well. And, Malcolm succeeded my husband as pastor of our church in Winter Park.

One day, Mary did something for me that was life-changing, and to date, I never told her what a profound effect she has had on my life:

Prior to Mary and Malcolm moving to the Winter Park/ Orlando area, they spent a weekend in our home as Malcolm was invited to facilitate the kick off of an evangelistic weekend at the church. This was the first time we had seen the Taylors since leaving Oakwood. I was so excited; I could not wait to see Mary. When Mary and Malcolm arrived, and I greeted Mary, the first thing she said to me was, "Marcia, are you still chewing up people and spitting them out?" And she said it with a smile. That question brought me to my knees that night, and I asked God to change me, not later, but right now! If during the five years after college, the primary thing that my friend could remember about me was that I chewed up people, then I was really not a nice person. That experience changed my life, and I have not been the same since.

I thank God that my change from being extremely antagonistic to now being more accepting, accommodating, and tolerant of others was initiated by the words of a friend. "Mary, I will be forever grateful!"

Forever friends: **Betty and Terry Giles**. Betty McDonald and Terry Giles were, and are, five years our junior. Inasmuch as my late husband never met a stranger, I had been accustomed to meeting people and keeping them as strangers, because I was very selective of my friends. If people I met seemed like they were not going anywhere in life or were not my age, I did not want them hanging around. When Gene met Betty and Terry, he invited them to visit our home, and he suggested it would be good if I became friends with Betty. Well, I objected. All I knew about Betty then was that she was younger than I was, and that was all I needed to know to conclude that there was no possibility of a friendship between us. However, when I met this wonderful woman, there was seriousness about her that the other college females did not seem to possess. Betty's intelligence and compassion for people went far beyond her years. She was the eldest of seven children, and that said a lot about her intuitive nature.

Terry had a twin brother, and since Gene was a twin himself, they had that one thing in common—neither Betty nor I could figure out the other commonalities, but since they were both theology majors that could have been the glue. Gene and Terry became close life-long friends, and so did Betty and I. However, it was not until after Betty and Terry were married, after graduation from college, and while both our husbands interned together at the Allegheny West Conference that our friendships matured.

I remember when we would have convocations in Columbus, Ohio, Betty and Terry would come in from Virginia and stay at our town home. I was always anxious to see Betty so we could do our "sister things" and especially exchange recipes and talk about fashion. One weekend when Betty arrived, I showed her all the fancy shirts and ties I had purchased for Gene, and then I displayed the two dresses I had *made* for myself. Betty's response to my two home-made dresses really hurt my feelings as she said, "Now, Marcia, look at all the garments of exceptional quality you have purchased for Gene so he can look good, and you are going to this event looking homemade. We have got to do something about this!" Betty further added that our hus-bands would always look nice—even with the same suit—if they only changed shirts and ties, and that we could do the same. So, off we went to the mall where I purchased my first two tailored suits, four blouses, two scarves, a belt, two pairs of shoes, and a brand-named hand bag. Betty was already *hooked up* with her outfits. Thus began a new and lasting dress style for me. I thought I was making a fashion statement in wearing homemade dresses, but this new style was far superior. I have never worn an ordinary dress since. Every time Betty visited, there was something new and last-ing to remember.

It was at AU, during our seminary years, that Betty and I (and Gene and Terry) had a lot of time to spend together. It was at AU that Betty gave birth to our goddaughter, Toyin. "Toy" and our sons grew up like brothers and sister. We lived off campus, as usual, and Betty and Terry lived on campus. There were times at AU when we were so broke that Betty and I would call each other to find out what we had in our houses to eat. Betty, the vegetarian, would say, "We have some beans and some collard greens." Then, I would add, "We have some cornbread and some white potatoes!" and together we'd say, "Let's do dinner!" Then one of us would ask, "Our house, or yours?" It was usually at our house since seminarians loved to be off campus. Together, our families would dine like kings, queens, princess, and princes.

The most memorable times with Betty that I have se-lected to share in this book are the times when I would wake up on a Sabbath morning in Michigan, look out the window at the two or three feet of snow on the ground, and tell the kids that we wouldn't be going to church today. The boys would be so sad, that they would just sit at the window to see if "Aunt Betty" and Toy were passing by on their way to the campus church, Pioneer Memorial. Almost without fail, they would see Betty and Toy trudging through the snow and heading to our house. Oh, the glee on their faces, and the shout, "Mom, here comes Aunt Betty and Toy. We are going to church today!" Then Betty would come in and give me the *third degree* because the kids were not dressed. She would get busy, grabbing their clothes and boots and trying her best to get them dressed so they would not be late for Sabbath School. Of course, seeing her determination and commitment to having the children in church and in their classes, made me feel so badly. I eventually had to get moving and dressed as well. Those days paid off for our children, and I appreciate Betty for her persistence.

Today, neither Betty nor I are married to our first husbands. I am unmarried, and Betty is remarried to a wonderful man—**Willie Anderson**—and they have a son, Aman. Willie has been spun into this wonderful, friendship and has truly been a friend to me as well. He did something for me that he had never done for anyone else. After Gene died, he cosign on a lease for my first car because I could not stand alone as a single-income female with the finance company.

Betty, who is now Mrs. "Jean" Anderson and residing in Orlando, Florida, is the best friend I have ever had—and the one friend I did not want to have. We have journeyed down similar paths since our early 20s, and family members often describe us as Lucy and Ethel from *I Love Lucy*, Louise and Helen from *The Jeffersons*, or Gayle and Oprah from *O*.

Through the love of our college friends, we have become members of a global family who continue to share, nurture, and encourage. Even after Gene's death, these individuals continue to be faithful and dear family members.

Fragrance of God's Love

Chapter 5

ROBERT

Robert T. Smith, PhD, and my husband were classmates—both in college and at the seminary. They were both very active on campus. I had seen Robert often but had spoken with him very little. I would acknowledge his presence when we were in close proximity, but during the years in school, we had never had a full-length conversation.

Like my husband, he was very agile and stable—especially for someone who was unmarried while in college. Robert appeared to have had a lot going for him in his youth, and I believe that was the reason I really did not have an affinity toward him. It seemed he was born with a *silver spoon* in his mouth, as he always wore the best in clothes and was able to travel anywhere in the world his heart desired. He was also a third generation clergyman. His father and uncle held executive positions in "the work," and I felt Robert had received special privileges that the other hard-working pastors had not received. He spent no time in the field as a pastor of local congregations. It appeared he was promoted to an administrative position in the regional office much too quickly, and that bothered me.

Several years had passed since school. My family was now living in Florida, and I was working for the federal government. While working for the FDIC my travel within the US was extensive. Employees were often on assignment to metropolitan areas for weeks and even months. Consequently, I was blessed to have been able to stay in grand hotels and enjoy fine dining—no complaints. In almost every city I visited, my husband and I knew someone from his school years with whom I could visit, converse with, or go out with while I was on detail for the federal government.

One day as I was preparing for another trip out of town—a three-week detail, Gene was in our family room going through his *little black book* to see who lived in that town that he knew would be willing to watch out for me while I was there—take me to lunch, converse about old times, or take me on a sightseeing journey. Well, there was absolutely no one I knew in that city, and I did not believe my husband knew anyone their either.

However, before long, he was speaking on the telephone with Robert: "Hey man, my wife is coming to Atlanta for three weeks. Do you think you would have any time to show her around town?" I assumed the answer was yes, as Gene was very happy when he returned to the bedroom. (I was very unhappy.) My question: "Of all the people in the world, why did you have to call him?" It was then that I confided in my husband, letting him know I had never "liked" that man and didn't think I ever would. As usual, Gene called it what it was. He said, "Sweetheart, you have been jealous of him all this time for no reason. Live, and let live, and set yourself free."

After my third evening in Atlanta, locked in my hotel room after abruptly ending my *fun time* evening with some of my coworkers, I finally broke down and called Robert. The next day we had lunch. There began my acquaintance with Pastor Robert T. Smith, and our subsequent lifelong friendship. I told Robert that day how I had felt about him all these years. "Not that my disdain kept me up nights," I said, "I just did not want to know you." Well, that day my ignorance was dispelled, and I became acquainted with one of the most wonderful men I have ever known.

I learned that every summer when Robert was not in school, he worked from city to city canvassing neighborhoods and selling Christian magazines and books. I ascertained that some of his trips overseas were what he worked for or that were gifted to him because of his hard work. I discovered that he was truly a people person and not a snob. It seemed every service agent in Atlanta knew Robert by name, and he knew them. He was pleasant and courteous and exuded with a temperament that was very becoming to one of God's servants. What I enjoyed most that afternoon was learning of some of Robert's travels. I did not know he had visited every major city in the world, and as I prodded him to speak about his trips to cities in Africa, Brazil, Australia, and China, I found myself living vicariously through his journeys.

I returned to Florida forgiven, refreshed, and set free, all because my unwarranted prejudice toward Robert had been eradicated. When I told my husband how this trip had changed my feelings toward his friend, he asked, "Now, don't you feel better?" And, I did. In large convocations when districts and conferences would gather, I would see Robert on occasion—he was a mover and a shaker.

I never thought I would ever live in Atlanta, Georgia, but a year after my husband's death, the FDIC office in Orlando relocated there, and I was one of the few support staff selected in the transfer. Even though Robert and I lived in the same city then, we seldom ever saw each other. He and his wife, Ann, were socialites, and, of course, Robert was the world traveler. On one occasion after dining out with some friends from work, I saw Robert driving down the street. He stopped, parked his car, and came out to greet me and my coworker "Cheryl." She was so amazed at how beautifully dressed he was, and she fell in love with his fancy car. As usual, Robert was on the run and so were we; so we spent only a few moments in introductions, and he was off again.

While living in Atlanta, I saw and met some beautiful people and was exposed to the true ethnicity of African Americans. Sure, I had lived in New York City; Huntsville, Alabama; Washington, DC; Columbus, Ohio; Berrien Springs, Michigan; Winter Park, Castleberry, Orlando, Tampa, Clearwater, and Daytona Beach, Florida; but associating with African Americans in those cities did not compare to the exhilaration of being a resident of Atlanta. It was there that African American heritage was not only studied, but lived.

It was in Atlanta that I met proud, assertive, and affluent individuals. It was in the FDIC office in Atlanta that one of my coworkers, realizing how little I knew about Black people, asked, "Marcia, where have you been? Living under a rock?" I realized then that being born and reared in Jamaica, West Indies, where there was no segregation because of racial distinctions, and having been a pastor's wife with only an idiomatic clerical focus, kept me sheltered from a lot of political and social issues concerning our people. Now, as a resident of this wonderful city, I was not going to be sheltered anymore. I would learn all that I could while living in Atlanta about my people and about the world.

It was in Atlanta that I felt the loneliness of being single. I remember one evening after our church's youth program ended that it was announced that there was going to be a basketball game after sunset. Families and couples were excited about this social event, but I was not. I suddenly felt alone and rushed to my car before others could see my tears. That evening as I drove home, I could hardly see the road not only because of my tears but because of the heavy rainfall. During that journey, I asked the Lord why I had to be alone when all around me others were having fun with family members and/or significant others. Then the answer came: *"I left the portals of heaven."* It was then that I realized how lonely Christ must have felt when he came to this earth, away from His Father and all the heavenly angels, to be the propitiation for our sins. At that point, I dried my tears and continued my ride home with a spirit of sobriety. When I arrived and opened the door to my apartment, I confronted an atmosphere of brightness that I had never before seen in my home, and I felt that angels welcomed me there. I knew then that God was compassionate to my feelings, sensitive to my needs, and nearer to me than any human being could ever have been that night.

My tenure in Atlanta only lasted for a short time. (In a subsequent chapter, you will learn why.) I eventually moved away from Atlanta, and away from where my friend Robert lived. But it did not matter, because I realized that friends are friends regardless of their geographical locations or the frequency or infrequency of contact.

Robert

This chapter will end with the most wonderful story about my friend Robert:

It was the end of the month. I had faith that my payroll earnings, which were automatically deposited in my checking account, were there and that I could pay my bills in the same fashion I did from month to month. With this confidence, I mailed a check to my landlord even before the payroll date. Other bill payments, however, would usually go out after I had actually received my written payroll statement, but my rent payment was always mailed in time for delivery to the business office before the third day of the next month. After sending out my rent check, I opened my payroll statement and discovered that only one-third of my expected income was deposited in the bank. What a shock! What was in the bank was not even enough now to cover the check I had already mailed to pay my rent. I immediately got on the telephone to Washington's Office of Personnel Management (OPM) to find out what had happened. To my amazement, I discovered that the IRS (Internal Revenue Service) had taken one thousand six hundred dollars from me, and I was assured that another eight hundred dollars would be extracted on the next pay period. What was I supposed to do? I was a widow living on my own; I had a son at Oakwood College whose tuition and room and board needed to be paid; I had another son in Orlando who was depending on me for some financial assistance; and the amount in the bank was not enough to cover my rent check. In addition, I needed food, gasoline, and, most of all, peace of mind. I knew I needed to hire a Certified Public Accountant (CPA) to get my money back from the IRS, as they surely were wrong in their claim. I also needed some immediate funds—if not to pay my other bills, then certainly to cover my rent.

After getting off the telephone with OPM, I contacted a CPA who was willing to look at my tax records. The next day I took the necessary paperwork to his office and after a brief review, he assured me that he could help me and I would not have to pay him until the matter was resolved. My CPA also assured me that when he completed the refund paperwork, the IRS would be indebted to me for all they had deducted and with interest.

I then took a trip to the management office of my apartment complex and explained to them what had happened. They had not yet received my rent check, and I told them that if they attempted to cash it the check would not clear. They reminded me of our lease agreement and told me I had ten days to come up with the rent monies.

A few days later at work, I confided in my coworker Cheryl about the dilemma I was in. Her response, "Marcia, quit tripping! What about your rich friend Robert? Why don't you ask him to lend you some money? He sure looks like he is good for it."

"No! No! No!" I responded. "I could never borrow from anyone—certainly not Robert. I don't know him that well, and I certainly do not want to know him that well. Never! Never! Never!"

When I returned home from work that evening, there was a note on my door from the management office. It was a notice of pending eviction. I had seven days in which to come up with the rent, or I would be put out of my apartment. All I could do was pray. I did not want to do anything else. Sure, I had my sisters and brother, but they had families and responsibilities of their own. I surely did not want to bother them about my financial woes. So, I prayed. As I finished praying, the telephone rang. It was Robert. When I answered the telephone, he said, "Marcia, I am in the Virgin Islands, and you said you had family here. Would you give me their name and telephone number?"

I said, "Of course!" And I gave him my sister Clover and brother-in-law Elroy's name and telephone number. Robert then asked what was wrong, as I did not sound like myself. I told him nothing was wrong, but he did not believe me. After some persuasion, I finally told him what I was going through. He then said, "I should be back in the states within a few days, and I will see what I can do to help. I'll call you. Bye!"

Likely story! I figured that would probably be the last time I would hear from Robert, and I felt I had embarrassed myself by letting him know I was in need. Days went by. Nothing changed. I did not hear from Robert, and I did not call him, even though Cheryl kept urging me to do so. The day before I was to be evicted, I came home to find the expected notice. I retrieved the envelope that

Robert

was taped to my front door by the apartment manager and laid it on the dining table. Then I proceeded to fix my supper. I broiled the last vegetarian patty and baked the last potato I had in the apartment. When it was time to go to bed, I said a prayer, and then I opened the envelope from the property management. When I unfolded the enclosed letter, there were three words that seemed to be illuminated: "Paid in Full." My rent had been paid by my friend Robert!

There are numerous stories I could probably have written about Robert, and perhaps there are numerous people who have had similar, wonderful exchanges with this man of God, but I have chosen never to forget this experience because it reminded, and reminds, me that my debt to sin was **paid in full** by Jesus when I did not deserve it, did not earn it, but truly needed His sacrifice.

For many years, I kept this deed of kindness to myself at Robert's request, but before this book was published, I received his approval to tell this story. Thank you, my friend!

Through Robert's love, I understand that friends are who they are and not who we make them out to be, and that *a friend [when you are] in need is truly a friend indeed.*

Chapter 6

MY DIVORCE

Divorce! A word I was always afraid to use in my vocabulary, because its meaning was something I never wanted for my life. I was brought up believing that marriage was forever—*'till death do you part*—and that there was no exception to the rule. I never thought it would happen to me or that I would ever be able to write on or talk about the experience. But, here I am—knowledgeable, able, and willing.

My widowhood lasted approximately three years. During that time, I did not fully accepted singleness, because I wanted to be physically intimate again with a husband. I was married to my first husband for so long, and I loved being married and treasured the beauty of marriage. There was something comfortable and protective in a marital relationship that I could not find in singleness. To me, marriage was the canopy of moral protection.

Six months after my husband's death, God urged me to develop, and include, a singles presentation in our seminars ministry. However, in spite of the fact that I was involved in teaching men and women how to be happy singles, through the ministry of *The Complete Woman/Man Seminars*, I envisioned that one day I would be married again. So engrossed with that thought, I had purposely overlooked how God had, and was, taking care of me during these times. How when I did not have, He provided through unexpected and miraculous ways; how when I was alone, he lighted up my life; how when I became despondent, he allowed a facility to call for seminar services. He had been a mighty good God to me, but deep down, I "knew" or "felt" He could not satisfy my physical needs.

Since God knows our thoughts, and because He loves us so much that He will grant the desires of our heart, He gave me what I yearned for: a mate. Shortly after moving to Atlanta, I received a call from a girlfriend in Tennessee who said she had someone she wanted me to meet. She asked if she could give him my telephone number. I told her I was not interested. She went on to say great and wonderful things about him, and I still was not interested (especially since this man was 60 years old, and I was only in my early 40s). My friend and I continued to talk for much longer than we should have, only because she wanted me to say yes to her request. Finally, I said, "OK, give him my number, but please ask him not to call me after 9:00 p.m. as I go to bed very early." After a short telephone courtship and a few visits back and forth from Ft. Lauderdale, where he lived, we were married. I quit my job with the FDIC in Atlanta and moved back to Florida.

I was remarried not only for companionship, but I had hoped that my second husband would be a good step-dad (a wise counselor) for my children and a provider. There were numerous individuals who thought I should not get re-married, including my sons. I remember one day my son Eugene called me from Oakwood College and said, "Mom, I met a lady today who knows the man you are going to marry, and she said to tell you don't do it! This guy is a philanderer!" I remember chuckling to myself before I answered him. Then, I said, "Gene, he may have been (and was) in his younger years, but this man is 60 years old, I am sure he is now over it—as he has stated." Needless to say, my son was so disappointed, but I truly thought I was doing the right thing. So, I did not listen to any wise counsel, because I knew God had provided this man for me. And He did, but God wanted me to learn a lesson that I would never, ever forget. I thus entered the marital school of hard knocks.

Going into the marriage, we each had stipulations. Mine was that my then fiancée was never to interfere with my friendships, my ministry, or my sleep. Of course, he said he would honor that request. Friendships, ministry, and an adequate amount of rest were important and "sacred" to me. Friends kept me encouraged, ministry kept me focused and committed, and sleep allowed me to function at my maximum potential. Needless to say, these were the three areas that were encroached on throughout the marriage.

My second marriage lasted approximately four years; however, we lived together for only two and a half years. The first two years of that second marriage were a blissful time for me. I loved this man with every fiber of my being, with the love that only God could have given. He was several years older than me and that ensured a certain degree of respect that no other man had ever received from me.

Gradually I began to notice that my mate was disrespecting me. At every opportunity, he tried to discredit me in public; he treated me like a child and tried to isolate me from my friends and family. It appeared that the things he admired in me, at first—my popularity, my independence, and my integrity—were the very things he hated after we were married. I remember once telling him that there was no man—to be born, yet living, or dead—who could ever destroy my self-esteem. But, I gradually became very unhappy in our marriage.

One weekend my son Eugene drove down from college for a brief visit. When he was about to leave, I almost begged him to take me back to Alabama. But, I pretended to be happily married so he would not have to worry about his mother. Before my son left, he gave me a present. It was a wall calendar with an inscription that read "Where there is life, there is hope." I knew God had allowed him to give me that gift, but I never knew if he sensed my heavy burden, and I did not ask.

At the end of our second year of marriage, I knew I was in an unequal union. I had forced the hand of God to put me in a relationship in which I was dying—spiritually, physically, and emotionally. My only way out was to pray sincerely for God to intervene, and I did. One night, God gave me a very horrific, but prophetic dream:

The Prophetic Dream

In the dream two hands picked me up from the place where I stood with my husband. (What made the dream so horrific is that we were both frogs.) When I realized I was being lifted away from him, I turned my head to look back, and I saw that my husband was in a cloud of darkness and as he looked up, his eyes were blood red, and he had suddenly become dark and bloated. As these hands slowly lifted me, I observed (from an outside imagery) that there was a straight line in the center of my back. The back side of me nearest to the place my husband stood was completely black, and my left side was brightly lit. There were three separate rays (sources) of brightness coming from the left side, reflecting on only half of my body.

While being held by these large unflinching hands, I proceeded to bend and reach to my right to pull my husband up along with me. But the hands would not acquiesce. I started to cry and asked, "Why won't you let me pick my husband up?" There was no answer. Then I asked, "May I turn to the left and see from where these bright lights are being generated?" The answer: *"No! I have only allowed you a peripheral view, because if you look into the light you will be blinded."*

When I awoke from my dream, the ribs on my right side were in terrible pain. My right ribs hurt for seven consecutive days, and I believed that in my dream I had wrestled with God.

I knew now that my marriage was finished, but I did not want it to end—I just wanted it fixed. Since I never wanted to experience the stigma of a divorce, like Moses, I asked God to take my life instead. But deep down in my soul, I knew I would live to face the awkwardness of having taught others how to improve the quality of their family life and mine was now falling apart.

For two weeks I prayed and asked God to give me the full interpretation of this dream, and He did. I was shown that it was time to get packing. God wanted me to know that He was lifting me out of this relationship but that I was coming out partially and permanently stained—my domestic life, that which my ex-husband had touched, and my ministry would now and forever be a dichotomy.

After being shown this interpretation, I was disappointed that my domestic life would be tainted, but I also knew that there was hope in the fact that there would be great blessings through three glorious sources that God had prepared for me.

I know now that the sources were: (1) the writing of my first inspirational book, (2) our media broadcast and Internet ministry: "Fragrance of God's Love," and (3) my ministry as a hospital chaplain.

The next six months that I remained in my marriage was sheer hell. The blinders were off. God allowed my eyes to be opened to see my husband as he really was, and it was frightening. The philanderer's spirit had not died, and I was indeed married to a philanderer and a gigolo. As my husband continued to get uglier and uglier (inside and out) and blatantly violated our marriage, I finally told him the dream God had showed me. This only made him angrier. He started to tell everyone who would listen that I thought I was better than he was. During that time, the Holy Spirit continued urging me to pack my clothes. (Ironically, my clothes were all that was unpacked during the time I lived with this man. All the other containers I brought back to Ft. Lauderdale from Atlanta were never opened.) I could never figure out why I could not bring myself to open my other boxes that had aligned the walls of our garage, but now I knew. However, I did not start packing or retain a mover until the last two weeks of my sojourn in my ex-husband's house.

Two weeks before my scheduled departure from the home, while at work for the Social Security Administration, Office of Hearings and Appeals, my supervisor Von came to my desk and told me there was a police officer in the lobby waiting for me to come out. She said, "Marcia, I think too much of you to have allowed him to come into the office, so I have asked the officer to wait outside." Well, I knew I had not committed a crime, so I curiously made my way to the lobby of our building. That day I discovered I had been forced out of our home under a restraining order from the Broward County Court.

That evening, I was escorted to my residence by a police officer and was told I had approximately twenty minutes to take from the house any personal items that I would need, including clothes for work, until the court hearing, which was in ten days. As I threw my valuable clothing, shoes, toiletries, etc. into the trunk of my brand-new automobile, for which I did not need a cosigner, it was with swiftness. Not only because I was under time constraints, but because I felt the evil emanating from the home and from being in the presence of mine enemy who was standing by, watching with blood-shot eyes.

As I drove the fifteen miles to my sister's home in Miramar, Florida, my vision was blurred with tears, but I was probably the happiest woman on the road that night. I was happy, because I knew God loved me enough to release me from a marriage in which I was faithful—there was no guilt. I knew beyond a shadow of a doubt that He had rescued me, and I was as free as a bird to soar. I actually felt as though I had just been released from prison.

When I arrived at my sister's and brother-in-law's home in Miramar that evening and asked if I could stay with them for a little while, they were more than happy to accommodate me for as long as I needed to stay. I sat by the side of my sister's bed and told her only about the restraining order. Then my sister Norma, who was a cancer survivor, cursed.

I had never heard my sister curse before. Not Norma! She was the *good* sister—the most religious and the most sensitive. I realized then how broken she was for me and that I could not tell her any more about my sordid life with this man. My sister made another statement that night that I will never forget. She said, "I have suffered now 32 years with cancer, but I would never trade this for what you are going through tonight." What she was actually saying was that she could not image her husband, **Claudius Bromfield**, who had accepted her "for better or for worse" treating her that way. And, she had had cancer all the years of their marriage. What a loving husband my sister had!

When I finally read the restraining order, I learned that my husband had accused me of "trying to kill him by poisoning his food." Of course, his allegation was unfounded, and the court case was dismissed. But that day, the day I was served at my job, was one of the most humiliating days of my life. I did not know my ex-husband could have stooped so low, but when one is under the direction of evil spirits, there is nothing he or she will not do. I called my friend **Audrey Ware** from work the day I was served, and she suggested I hire an attorney. I retained a lawyer that very day who represented me in court the day of the restraining order hearing and who also proceeded with the divorce.

When I visited my attorney's office in preparation for the filing of my divorce petition, the consultation was done by a female attorney who was his assistant. She asked the unavoidable question, "What has brought you to this decision?" When I told her of different occurrences during my six-month ordeal, she broke down and cried. I did not truly realize how abusive my life with this man had become until I saw the reaction of my sister, and now, this attorney. So, I have refrained, even in this book, from telling the gruesome details of my marital turmoil. They are being withheld to protect the innocent as well as the guilty. My ex-husband is a father himself, and I grew to love my step-children and their mother, his ex-wife. I have often thought that if I had taken time out to befriend his ex-wife (who was then remarried) I would have been spared a lot of grief. When I met her and saw that she was a woman of class that any man would have wanted to marry and keep forever, I was convinced that the problem in his first marriage was not his wife, as he had wanted me to believe, but the problems were with him.

Even though I had no history with this man—no children, no property, no shared assets, and suddenly no more love for him, being single again and facing the embarrassment of a divorce was hard. I went through all the emotions of a dissolved relationship in which all was given and not much was given back.

After I had mended and was eventually healed from my divorce, I had two questions for God. The first was, "Why did my husband turn on me so viciously?" God showed me it was because I had told him the dream; just like the Biblical story of Joseph and his brothers, the dream made my ex-husband jealous and insecure, and this was the reason he wanted me gone. I then asked God why my enemy had gotten so fat and dark and bloody-eyed in the dream, and He said, *"Because he is full of unlived doctrinal knowledge and there is (and was) no light in him."* God had allowed me to be duped by someone who was only an instrument in His hands. He allowed my husband to be the "Judas" in this relationship—to bring it to an end and to cure me of my quest for any other man but God himself.

I spent six beautiful months living with my sister and brother-in-law. Little did I know those would have been the last six months with my sister Norma. Even through this disaster, God blessed us with these precious months together. I was able to accompany my sister to doctor's appointments; I saw first-hand the depth of her husband's love for her; and each week we did three-way calling with our sister Clover, at times we included our brother, Keith. We talked about old times and the wonderful love of God. My siblings were especially pleased that God had rescued me from an unwholesome union. My brother never met my ex-husband. This was a good thing, as my brother would not have been comfortable in the presence of anyone who he knew was taking advantage of any of his sisters.

My Divorce

I never thought I would be thankful for a failed marriage and subsequent divorce, but I am. I will share three reasons why I am thankful.

First, God used this situation to show me that disobedience and sin have built-in consequences. Did my marriage fall into this category? It most certainly did! Seven years after my divorce, I prayed and asked God if there was anything between me and Him that I needed to ask forgiveness, and He said, *"You need to ask me to forgive you for your remarriage."* What an indictment! But what a joy it was to have received that forgiveness. Then God told me, *"If I wanted you married, I would not have allowed your first husband to die."*

Secondly, I am thankful to have had not only the experience of the divorce but the knowledge of being evicted and deeply hurt by one who took a vow to love and protect. This first-hand experience has empowered me with compassion for those who have endured like incidences.

Thirdly, I have learned that even though the Scriptures declare, "...What therefore God hath joined together, let not man put asunder" (Matthew 19:6 [KJV]), <u>God</u> can, and will, put asunder a marriage that is not pleasing to Him at any time and in any way He desires. But, we need to be sure that the separation is being orchestrated by God. When God is the originator, there is no stigma or guilt for the one who has sought His divine guidance.

Through my divorce, God rescued me from a physical and emotional death and revealed to me that He permitted the remarriage and He also initiated the divorce. I thank God for my freedom!

Chapter 7

IVORY

Ivory Jackson and I became acquainted while we were both living in Florida. She was a pastor's wife as well, and we spent a lot of professional time together. We saw each other at conferences, camp meetings, weddings, funerals, and at times when her husband was a guest pastor in my husband's church.

When my late husband became terminally ill, she and her husband, **Pastor S. J. Jackson**, would travel miles from their home in Altamonte Springs, Florida, to Daytona Beach just to pay a home visit. I remember one evening they came to our home quite unexpectedly when Gene and I were dealing with a gut-wrenching situation; all we could do was sit on the floor of our living room and lament. When the Jackson's gained entrance to our house, they found us still in that position, and they got down on the floor with us. This couple ministered to us, our sons, and other family members in a way that only they could do.

It was a year after my late husband's passing, when I was living in Atlanta, that I saw Ivory at *The Complete Woman/ Man Seminars* at which I was presenting. I had an engagement to facilitate two workshop sessions for the Southeastern Conference Women's Retreat at a hotel in Daytona Beach. I was flying in to meet our vice president, and my friend, Jean, as we were the consultants on this particular assignment. Jean and I had agreed to share a hotel room and this took some doing, as both our preferences were to have separate rooms. The day before our arrival and registration, I received a call from Ivory. She wanted to know if she could room with me. She had not pre-registered before the deadline and was unable to obtain a room at this late date. *"No way,"* I thought. *"It is bad enough that I must share the room with one individual; now three in a room?*

No way; no how!" So, I politely responded to Ivory by saying, "Jean and I are rooming together, so let me pay her the courtesy of calling to see if this will be alright with her. I will call you back." I was trying to pass the buck. When I called Jean and told her that Ivory wanted to room with us, she was excited. She thought this would be great, and then she added, "There must be a reason for this, Marcia; don't be so close minded." Well, I gritted my teeth and called Ivory back. What could I say but that it was all right? Ivory and Jean were excited, and reluctantly, but eventually, I warmed up to the idea.

As usual, Jean was right. There was a God-ordained reason that we were together in such close proximity. That weekend was the most wonderful weekend I had ever spent with three in a room. At the end of the conference, we hardly wanted to go our separate ways. Thus began the wonderful friendship between me and my friend Ivory.

Ivory has always been a pleasant person and always has a smile. She would bring me to laughter at the craziest times in my life—times when I would rather cry than laugh. I remember the time, before moving to Atlanta, when I had to do my first seminar presentation after my late husband's death at a church where he was their former pastor. For some reason, I was nervous beyond explanation. I had gotten dressed for the program; had all my material together; was determined to be on time; but felt so uneasy I could not put it into words. I had to pass Ivory's house en route to the church and something just made me stop. I rang her door bell, and Ivory opened the door with the biggest, brightest smile I had ever seen. At that very moment, my nervousness was quelled. It seemed her smile made all the difference in the world. When she asked why I had stopped, I told her I wasn't sure but I was off now to do the seminar. It took just a smile from Ivory to give me the encouragement I needed, and God lead me to her door that evening.

It was Ivory who stood by my side again as I went through those dreadful last six months in my ex-husband's home. We were then living sixteen miles apart—I in Ft. Lauderdale, and she in Miramar. The things I could not share with Jean, or even with my sisters and brother, I shared with Ivory. Satirically, it was at the Jackson's home that my ex and I had our Florida wedding reception and where we received the blessing of her family and some of our friends. She was so excited for me when I got remarried; and she was so heartbroken for me when she saw how our marriage came to its abrupt end.

During that emotional time of our breakup, Ivory stood by my side, and she had a prophetic message. When God took off my rose-colored glasses so much was revealed to me at one time that I almost fainted under the spell. God took pity on me and did not give me more than I could bear. So, He told me there were still three other things I needed to know but that I was not ready to hear them. When I was ready, He would allow Ivory to disclose the three messages He had for me. I never told Ivory God had told me this. I never knew whether God had told it to her then or later, and I did not know whether it was good news or bad news. All I knew was that I could not take any more bad news or surprises.

Well, it was November 1998, two weeks before Thanksgiving. Both Ivory and I had driven from South Florida to do some visiting in Orlando. We had driven up together to visit with my son Jon and her son Kit. Then, before going back to Miramar, we stopped to visit with Jean. As we stood outside Jean's home saying our good-byes, something made me say to Ivory, "Girl, God told me a few months ago that you have three things to tell me, I am ready to hear them now." Ivory started smiling and jumping up and down. Then she said, "I was wondering when you were going to ask."

Without any hesitation she blurted out the following: (1) You are going to be leaving Florida to live in Colorado Springs with your son Eugene, and he will be the one to ask you to come, (2) ... (I have refrained from mentioning the second prophecy because it directly involves my children and this is their story), and (3) your other son Jonathan will be coming a bit later to live with you in Colorado as well. Everything that God said would happen did happen!

Going to live in Colorado was hard to accept at first, as I never wanted to live in another state with cold winters. I hoped that my son and his family would get tired of the cold and move to Florida or someplace warm and accommodating. Now, I had to move—leave my friends, leave my sister, and my wonderful job.

I had had the privilege of working with **Judge Ruben Rivera**, an administrative law judge for the Social Security Administration (SSA) in Ft. Lauderdale, after my remarriage. For two years I had been his judicial assistant, and I loved my job. When I was first hired to work with him, I was told by one of my coworkers that all eyes were on me because, as the newest person on the team, I should never have been assigned to this judge. He was the hardest worker; he had the lengthiest docket; and he produced the highest number of decisions. My coworker "Mike" further stated, "You will never be able to keep up unless you work on Saturdays like most of the other workers." Well, I assured Mike that I had never worked on the Sabbath, and that I would not now, or ever, have any intentions of doing so. Not only did I not labor at my secular employment on a Sabbath, but there were some Fridays and Mondays that I had to take leave time, as I traveled out of town on many weekends to do seminars. I am happy to say that during my employment at SSA there was never a decrease in Judge Rivera's docket, and he continued to maintain his quota of decisions. I know it was God, and God alone, who blessed and sustained me during this period of employment with the federal government, and He has continued to do so in every area of my life's work.

Within two months after Ivory told me God's prophecy, I was on my way to Colorado Springs. As my son and I drove in the rental truck with all my belongings and my car on a hitch, I felt like Abraham, going into a land that he knew not of. The only thing Abraham knew was that anywhere with God was where he wanted to be, and I adopted the same attitude. I had lived in Florida an aggregate of eighteen years, so moving to Colorado took me away from all that was familiar—and especially from Jean and Ivory, but I knew God had special plans that were unknown to me.

My first three years in Colorado were literally three years of "famine." As a widow, I had now become accustomed to brief periods of shortages, but three years! During this time, I became familiar with every "widow" story in the Bible, and I understood why God had such compassion for the fatherless and the widows. My favorite widow story is found in 2 Kings 4:1-7, which most closely depicts the circumstances in which my sons and I found ourselves. However, as our domestic life suffered, my ministry flourished. It was during this time that I wrote a book, started our radio broadcast, and became a hospital chaplain.

At the beginning of my sojourn in Colorado Springs, and after getting somewhat settled in, I knew it was time to go job hunting. I had left the highest paying job of my occupational involvement and now I wanted to find a comparable position. I also had to develop new clientele to continue doing seminars on the weekends, as we were not well known in the Midwest. I had seen an ad for a worker for the Fourth Judicial District, Office of Dispute Resolution (ODR), and I applied. After that first interview, seeing what I had to do and the meager salary being offered, I came home praying that I would not get the job and that God would give me something better. Well, when I returned home that afternoon and checked my voice mail it was from the Fourth Judicial District, and they wanted to hire me. I ended up taking the job, hoping it would only be temporary until I could find something better. It was the hardest job I had ever worked in my entire life, and I was now making fifteen thousand dollars less, per year, than my last employment. God never opened another door for me, so finally I became convinced that He wanted me to have that particular position. I worked in the ODR with individuals experiencing the same thing I had experienced in my divorce—I completely understood the emotions of the individuals going through a divorce or experiencing a restraining order separation.

I grew to understand that God had prepared me for this position. However, for the first time in my adult life, my expenses exceeded my income. The first six months were not as bad as the subsequent thirty months because I kept withdrawing from my savings, and my son helped me out by not charging me rent. Then he and his wife moved, and it was downhill from there. There were months when if I paid my rent, then I was unable to pay for my car and vice versa. If I paid the credit card's minimum payment, the car insurance, utilities, and bought groceries, then I couldn't make the car payment. There were mornings when I would get ready for work not knowing whether or not my car was still on the lot or towed away by the Miami Federal Credit Union. But, my car was always there. I often thought if I did not get another job, or if God did not perform a miracle, I was surely going to be homeless, carless, or both. Well, I did not get another job, and the only miracle I could see is that God sustained me through those difficult times.

I remember confiding in Ivory, Jean, and Clover about my improvised state of living. Jean would often say, "You are living through a God thing. Stay connected, and He will see you through." What she really meant was that I was in such a financial quicksand that only God could help me out. However, at times my two friends and my sister would try to help by sending cash intermittently to help out with gasoline for my car and food for my table.

I also remember one Thanksgiving in which I was totally alone, and I was blessed to receive one of the baskets that our church had prepared for the needy during the holiday season. Had I not received those few items of groceries, I would have had nothing to eat. What was so ironic about this whole fiasco was remembering the times when I would give my entire paycheck to my late husband at the Thanksgiving and Christmas seasons to help the Daytona Beach church purchase baskets for our community. Now, I was one of the needy, receiving handouts from our church. I was so incensed.

Ivory

What does this have to do with my friend **Ivory**? Well, she also played an important part in helping me survive.. It was one of those days when I truly believed my car had been repossessed. I was two months behind in my car payment. I certainly needed to make a payment or two from this month's salary, and if I did so, then my rent would not be paid. I finally decided to keep the car and lose the apartment. I was going to try being homeless if God would allow me to maintain my wheels and my computer. Doesn't sound very rational, does it? Of course not, but who is truly rational when they are going through unwelcome crucibles? That morning as I got in my car to go to work, I started pounding on the dashboard of the vehicle and crying. I asked God why I could not just be blessed with seven hundred dollars so I could pay my rent and get partially caught up on my car payments as well. As I was becoming delirious, a still small voice said to me, *"You don't have to yell; you don't have to get crazy; I'm sitting right here."* Then, I realized that God truly was with me, and He knew all that I was going through.

While at work that day, something kept urging me to go and check my post office box. I took a drive at lunch time and went to the box. Among some other mail was a greeting card from Ivory—another of her usual encouraging messages to help me along my journey. When I opened the card there was a folded American Express money order enclosed. I could see that Ivory had sent me a money order for seventy dollars. Well, I did not quite know what to do with that amount of money, so I placed the card and the unfolded money order back in the envelope and returned to the office. While at work, the Holy Spirit kept urging me to reopen the card. I finally did, and this time, I unfolded the money order. It was for seven hundred dollars. No way! Where did Ivory get that much money, and how did she know that I needed it? Then I realized she didn't, but God did.

I was so choked up, flabbergasted, and humbled, that I could not even call Ivory. All I could do was to send up a prayer of thanksgiving to God. A few weeks later, I mustered up the courage to call Ivory and explain to her just how on time, unexpected, and unpredicted her gift had been. Of course, I could not end our conversation without asking her how she was directed to do such a thing. She said God told her to do it. "But, how," I asked.

Then she said, "Marcia, I know you are not going to quit until you hear the whole story." Ivory told me she had purchased the money order to send to a family member who needed it. After purchasing the money order, but before mailing it, her family member called and said she no longer needed the money. Ivory said she had been carrying the seven hundred dollars in her purse for several weeks, even though the Spirit kept saying, "Send it to Marcia Armstead in Colorado Springs." Ivory said upon hearing the same directive for the third time, she finally addressed an envelope and mailed it to me.

Ivory asked me never to repay her, because she felt that one day I would be able to help someone else the same way she helped me. And it happened. About two years later, after God pulled me from my financial quicksand, I was able to pay my neighbor's rent with exactly the same amount after she had a stroke.

Through Ivory's love, in the best and the worst of times, I have learned that friends are forever. Distance, time, and circumstances cannot alter what God has ordained to be. I thank God for my wise, joyous, prophetic, and forever friend.

Chapter 8

YVONNE & JANICE

I met **Yvonne (Grimes) Irving** by telephone. She was a member of the church my son and daughter-in-law attended in Colorado Springs—Palace of Peace. Word had gotten around that I was moving to Colorado, and Eugene gave her my telephone number in Miramar. Yvonne called about two days before I was scheduled to leave Florida. She wanted to pray with me for my safe travel and smooth transition. We talked for a very long time about our individual ministries and her work in the church as family ministries director. I knew she was calling long distance, and I could not understand why she kept talking so long, but it was on her dime, so I did not worry. I only knew that none of my out-of-state friends would ever talk this long, so I concluded that Yvonne would not be in my friendship camp.

Knowing how skeptical I am about meeting people and acquiring new friends—especially via telephone—God allowed Yvonne to say something in our conversation that made me know she was to be my friend. Actually, the words were spoken right before our conversation ended; they were said in her prayer. She prayed for my children; and, her petition contained the very words I would have used in beseeching God's intervention for my sons, my daughter-in-law Kisha, and (then) my only grandson Eugene III. It was truly amazing that the words on Yvonne's lips were the words in my thoughts for my family. I was sold on this sister!

Having been convinced that Yvonne was soon to become a wonderful friend, I looked forward to meeting her upon my arrival in Colorado Springs.

Yvonne's personality and demeanor, as depicted over the telephone, were the same as in person. We developed a wonderful friendship, and we did a lot of things together. Under her family ministries umbrella, I assisted her as singles ministries leader, and we planned programs together. That was fun! When she stepped down as family ministries director at the church, she recommended me for the position.

At first, there were some struggles in our relationship. Yvonne always wanted me to do something in the church, and I would tell her I had not done that before, did not have time to do it, or did not have an interest in doing it. She always ruffled my feathers every time I would say, "Oh, I can't do that!" She would respond with, "Yes, you can!" At first it was annoying, but after a while I discovered that everything I was adamant about not being able to do, I later did.

There are several things I admire about Yvonne, and one of them is her way with people. She is a social worker by profession, and she has an innate, appropriate response to the expressed needs of individuals. During my first three years of famine and glory in Colorado Springs, Yvonne was one of the few individuals who knew about my unmet needs and wants and my successes in ministry. One Thanksgiving week, she invited me over to her apartment just to chitchat. I thought that was unusual, because I knew, just like myself, how busy she was. We did not have time for chitchatting. With the oversight of *The Complete Woman/Man Seminars*, my chaplain's duties, the radio program, and my regular eight to five employment at the courthouse, I was extremely busy, and so was Yvonne—she had her ministry, her work, and her college curriculum. Anyway, I went over to her home that Sunday evening, and in the midst of our visit, Yvonne excused herself and left the room. I assumed she was going to the laundry room. But not so! Yvonne had skillfully sneaked out of the dwelling with my car keys and seven bags of groceries, which I later found in the trunk of my car. These bags contained every item that one would need to prepare a Thanksgiving meal. At first I felt she was treating me like one of her social work clients—I was a bit disturbed, but then God empowered me to accept her gifts in love and appreciation, because everything I received, I had needed.

He said it was from Him, and not Yvonne. She was only the instrument.

As my association with Yvonne continued, I began to learn that she had a reputation in Colorado Springs as being a godly woman. On one Sunday afternoon, she and I went to a Parade of Homes. As we were passing a couple on the stairs, the gentleman paused. He had recognized Yvonne, but it seemed he had forgotten her name. Yvonne paused as well with a silent acknowledgment and recognition. As activities on the staircase came to an abrupt halt—with several of us paused on the stairs—accommodating this delayed movement in both directions, the man introduced Yvonne to his wife by saying, "Honey, I want you to meet a woman of God." What an acclamation! What a validation! I could not have said it better myself.

Sadly, after about a year and a half of having Yvonne as my running buddy, she graduated from college and moved out of state to complete her master's degree at Andrews University. She never returned to Colorado Springs, but we never lost contact. What was so surprising to me after Yvonne left Colorado was learning from others how she had also helped them and how wonderful a person she was. Actually, I felt as if I was her only friend and that I was the only one she had gone out of her way to assist. But, in talking to others who had been blessed by her ministry, I discovered that what Yvonne did for me was a minor thing compared to how she had helped others. The joy for me was the confidentiality that she maintained in her relationship with me and with others.

Through Yvonne's love, I have a greater understanding of true compassion and faithfulness. But most of all, I know how wonderful it is when the life one lives speaks louder than his or her words.

~~~~~~~~~~~~~~~

I also met **Janice Braithwaite** via telephone. She, as well, was given my telephone number in Miramar, and she too had called to pray for my road trip from Florida to Colorado. My first thought was, "These people in Colorado are really praying people, but let me go see what they are all truly about." Actually, it was a bit scary as I had never associated myself with such great women of faith and spiritual strength.

When Janice and I finally met, I was glad to know her. I met a very beautiful woman with two handsome sons. Janice is very petite and feminine, but she was in the military and is a physically and emotionally strong woman. I did not perceive that we had much in common—besides the fact that we were both single parents with two sons each. I often wondered why God had allowed her in my life or me in hers, as she and I appeared to be opposites in many areas. Our personalities are very, very different.

Janice and I seemed to spend more time praying than socializing. We would pray together for our children. There were times when we were not able physically, emotionally, or financially to help our sons or contribute to their livelihood, and Janice and I would lift them up to God in prayer. I remember once Janice prayed so agonizingly and faithfully for my children that as she prayed I could actually see angels positioning themselves around my young men. Oh, how grateful I was to know that there was another mother crying out for my children. Janice was one of the prayer warriors in our church, but there were times we did not pray for everyone. In our times of solitude, we prayed just for our children.

On one particular Tuesday evening, neither Janice nor I had gone to the weekly prayer service at our church. Instead, Janice called, and we talked for a little while. Then she started singing, and I joined in. Before we knew it, we had spent about an hour on the telephone singing hymns, reflecting on the goodness of God, praying, and testifying. This time together was better than any prayer service we could have attended with a collective body of believers. Oh, how blessed we were to have spent this time together. It was time ordained by God, and it was wonderfully indescribable.

After five years of knowing Janice, she lost her oldest son to a homicide, and I lost my youngest son, a year later, due to medical complications. Since the passing of our children, Janice and I have not been in close proximity. She travels quite a bit, and I have remained, more or less, stationary.

The most surprising thing about my association with Janice is that I recently discovered that we met about nineteen years ago. When she was pregnant with her first son, she and her husband had spent a weekend in our home in Tampa, but I guess this did not come to mind until God was ready for this remembrance to take place.

Through the love of my friend Janice, I know that bonds can be formed not by having similar personalities but in having similar life experiences.

Chapter 9

JUANITA

Before meeting my friend Juanita in Colorado Springs, I had met **Marcia Harris, M.D.**, while still living in Ft. Lauderdale. One day Marcia gave me a letter she had received from Nia Publishing, asking her to write a commentary for their proposed *Women of Color Study Bible* [KJV]. Marcia said, "Girl, you are the writer; why not try your hand at this." I eagerly accepted the challenge and responded to the directives in the publisher's letter. I wrote three articles. Two were accepted for publication and one article, "Huldah: Too famous to be Popular"—2 Kings 22, was actually printed.

When I arrived in Colorado Springs, along with my leather-bound copy of the *Women of Color Study Bible*, I received information that each commentator was being asked to contact local radio and television stations to promote the Bible. I called one television station and two radio stations and left messages. Only one radio host returned my call, and that was **Evangelist Juanita Johnson**. Juanita expressed an interest in doing a feature on her radio program at KWYD-AM. She arranged a luncheon appointment, and we met and talked, not only about the Bible but about the ministry of *The Complete Woman / Man Seminars*. Juanita agreed to do a full interview with me on her radio program, His Great Testimonies.

After the broadcast, Juanita asked if I had ever done radio and would I like to do radio. She received a negative response to both questions. But Juanita insisted, and she got me my first radio contract with KWYD-AM. The program was called *Fragrance of God's Love*. Unfortunately, and fortunately, I only did three broadcasts for that station. My program, along with several other contracts, was abruptly terminated by the station's owner. After ten months of waiting to be picked up by another station, Juanita and I contracted with KCBR-AM, Monument/Colorado Springs.

Juanita and I had the same desire to see men and women saved and active in the work of the Lord. Juanita is a natural born evangelist and preacher, and I am a teacher. Both of us recognize and respect each other's gifts. Juanita possesses something that I do not have, a spirit of discernment. She can always tell when something is not going quite right with me and that results in a luncheon appointment. We grew to be very good friends, and even though our ministries have taken us down different paths—beyond the walls of the church—we both have a wonderful love for the church.

There are numerous contributions Juanita has made to my life, but there are some in particular that I will never forget. To best explain these, I will share with you excerpts from a *Fragrance of God's Love* radio broadcast in which Juanita was front and center. This particular broadcast was titled "Healing."

It was February 2001. I was on my way to my place of employment in downtown Colorado Springs. As I waited at a stoplight, the motorist directly behind me slammed into my vehicle at about 40 miles per hour.

The injuries to my upper back and neck were real. After going through twelve months of various types of therapy to restore me to painless functioning—and after all the reports were in to the insurance companies—I was almost convinced that the pain in my neck would never go away.

One therapist, who gave me full-body massages, was able to relieve the pain that I suffered by day, but at night when I laid my head down, the pain in my neck was excruciating and continuous.

One of my doctors prescribed a cervical pillow, and I was resigned that this was the only comfort I would ever receive. Whenever I would travel to do workshops or to visit with family and friends, my cervical pillow accompanied me.

*My friend, **Ken Jaray**, who is an attorney, and who was aware of my plight, said, "Marcia, whenever you are* ready to negotiate with the insurance company, I will be standing by. If you need me, just say the word."

I remember telling him that because of the severity of my nightly pains, my offender's insurance company (which I will not name in this discourse) had better plan to pay me at least a million dollars for this injury—or come pretty close to this figure.

Deep down inside I knew that no amount of money— ten thousand, a million, or even ten million dollars—could compensate me for the suffering I had gone through for the past twelve months and would continue to go through for the rest of my life. Actually, I was more scared and concerned about my health than I was about being compensated for my injuries.

Well, the bargaining started. Would you believe the insurance company's first offer was only one thousand five hundred dollars? Well, it was. When I first received their letter, I thought it was a joke. No kidding! And, if it was not a joke, then someone must have left out two very important figures.

I called my attorney right away, and he said, "Marcia, I am not surprised. And I am familiar with that particular insurance agent (who I will anonymously call Jeff). Ken said, "This guy is notorious for skimping for the insurance company, but go ahead and counter. I will not get involved until the time is right."

In the meantime, I was desperate for money. We went back and forth with counter offers until the final offer from Jeff was three thousand dollars. Still frustrated, hurt, injured, and feeling like a victim of insurance rape, I said, OK, I am going to take this thing to court and have my attorney enter his appearance in my case.

I'm going somewhere with this "Healing" message today, and I want you to stick with me.

It was a Friday morning in December 2001. As I was driving to work, my eyes gazed upon my fuel gauge, and I realized that I was running on empty—no gasoline in my car, and no source to glean from to supply this need. I had been borrowing from Peter to pay Paul; Paul was broke again, and so was Peter. Where could I turn again, but to my Lord!

That morning I prayed and cried in my car. As I was beginning to cry, I heard God speak to me. He said, "My *child, I own the cattle upon a thousand hills. I have already sold one so that you can be sustained; go today, at lunchtime, to Jeff's office and pick up the three thousand dollars."*

At first I thought the Lord was playing games with me. *Lord, I don't believe you want me to settle for only three thousand dollars!* But, He wasn't kidding. That was the only way my gasoline tank would get filled up today and my bills paid. Well, I went to work that morning, and I called Jeff. I told him I would be coming to pick up my check at lunchtime, and in the same breath, I tried to negotiate for a higher amount. Of course, he said no.

Having only one hour for lunch, I quickly darted out of my building at noon, headed for my car, and hit the highway. During that twenty-minute drive, God spoke to me again. He said, *"When you accept that check and sign the disclaimer; I want you to do it with no regrets and no animosity. And I am preparing you now to do just that. Don't be upset with Jeff,"* He continued, *"because I care for those who are oppressed, and I will take care of the oppressors of my people."*

When I arrived at the insurance company, I gladly accepted the three thousand dollars check and left there praying that I would have enough gasoline to get to the bank, obtain some cash, and fill up my tank before returning to work.

At the bank's drive-through window, I was greeted by a teller I had never seen before. I gave her two deposit slips: one to my business account for a one-thousand-five-hundred-dollar deposit and the other for a deposit to my personal account for one thousand three hundred dollars. My change then, was to be two hundred dollars in cash.

As soon as the transactions were complete, the teller handed me two receipts, confirming the deposits, and an envelope with my change. When I pulled the envelope from the tray, it felt rather thick for <u>only</u> two hundred dollars, and I was a bit upset, thinking she had given me a lot of small bills, but because of my time constraints, I did not argue but went directly to the gasoline station. I opened the envelope with my change, took out twenty dollars, and paid the clerk for my fuel.

Then, I rushed off to work, hoping to return to my place of employment by 1:00 p.m. Unfortunately, I did not arrive back at work until 1:10 p.m. Fortunately, there was no one waiting for services, so the first thing I did was open the envelope I had received from the teller to count my change. I wanted to make sure I had one hundred eighty dollars in change and that she had not given me a lot of small denominations.

Lo and behold, when I counted the money, I found that the bank teller had given me back not two hundred dollars but one thousand seven hundred dollars. Obviously the receipt she gave me showing that one thousand five hundred dollars had been deposited in my business account was now in error, as she had actually given me back all of that money.

I immediately picked up the phone to call the bank. Then the Holy Spirit said, "Put the phone down. Think about what you are going to say. This young lady could lose her job as a result of this error."

I picked up the telephone again and called the bank. I was careful not to speak to a supervisor or anyone else who would be instrumental in having her lose her job. God worked it out, so I was directly patched through to "drive-through" where this young lady answered the phone. I started to tell her that I had been there about a half-hour ago and that there was an error made, but before I could finish, she said sobbingly, "Are you Ms. Armstead?"

Needless to say, she was so glad to hear from me, as she had recognized too late the mistake she had made, and did not know what to do about it. She said, "I gave you back one thousand five hundred dollars more than I should have, can you come back before 3:00 p.m. today so I can reconcile my records?"

I could not because of my lack of back-up at the office. I then suggested to her that she find a way to void the one-thousand-five-hundred-dollar deposit registered to my business account, and I would redeposit the same amount on Monday morning, and she said she would.

The subject of my message today is "Healing," and I know you are wondering where this story is leading. But I ask you to hold on and keep traveling with me here; we are going someplace with this story.

Well, that was Friday. The next morning was Sabbath, a day in which I am not in the habit of turning on my computer unless I am listening to Christian radio over the Internet. However, I was instructed by the Lord to go to my computer and write a letter to Jeff at the insurance company.

He said, "What happened to you yesterday at the bank was not for you, it was for Jeff, and I want you to write this story in a letter to him."

*Of course, I obeyed. I got right up and began my letter to Jeff, reminding him that I was in yesterday, against the advice of my attorney, to accept what I felt was an unfair settlement for my bodily injuries, but something happened after I left his establishment **that** God wanted me to share with him.*

In the second paragraph, I reiterated the story of my overpayment from the teller and subsequent developments. I knew there was to be a third paragraph to this letter, but I did not know how to close. So, I saved the document and waited for God to give me directions on the closing of this letter.

With the document partially finished, I proceeded to get dressed for church. While in my Sabbath school class that morning, one of the elders touched me on the shoulder and said, "Sister Armstead, one of your friends is here to see you and she was wondering if you would come outside to the lobby."

I was curious as to whom this friend was, but within seconds, I discovered it was none other than Evangelist Juanita Johnson. She said, "Marcia, God asked me to stop by today to let you know that the financial famine you have been encountering ever since you moved to this city is soon to come to an end. He said to take courage and know that anything He has done for you so far is only the tip of the iceberg. There is more to come."

Juanita started to leave, and then she turned around and gave me a book she had been holding in her hand. She said, "This is my devotional book, and as I was reading it this morning, God told me to bring it to you as there is something in this reading He wants you to see."

As I opened to the reading of the day, my eye focused on a quote by Jim Elliot, which I had heard before, but today, it was for me. He says, "He is no fool who gives what

*he cannot keep to gain what he cannot lose." After read-
ing this quote, I gave the devotional back to Juanita, and I
knew then just how the letter to Jeff should end.*

*That evening I retrieved the unfinished letter and
closed as follows: "Jeff, I felt good yesterday, not only
knowing that I had fulfilled my moral obligation, but that
I saved a teller's job by doing what was honest, fair, and
just. I have read, and I believe, that 'at the end of the day'
the only thing that matters is integrity. In conclusion, I join
in praise with Jim Elliot who wrote, 'He is no fool who
gives what he cannot keep to gain what he cannot lose'.
God bless you during this New Year!"*

*Yes, our subject today is about healing. Healing to
my severe, nightly neck pain came to me that night on
the wings of a dove through a telephone prayer. My friend
Juanita called me. After chatting for a while over the experiences of the weekend and her listening to me talk about
the pain in my neck, she said, "Marcia, let's pray for your
healing."*

*Juanita sent an earnest petition up to God for heal-
ing. She thanked Him for that healing and for the green
foliage He was allowing me to consume that was contrib-
uting to that wellness. I had not told my friend about the
Barley Life food supplement I had been taking. How did
she know? I knew then it was only a prophetic utterance.
I knew that demons trembled at the name of Jesus that
night, because the power in His name had healed me.*

*That night I went to bed. I placed my head on the cer-
vical pillow that I had used every night over the past year
and did not know what to expect. What I did not expect
(throughout the period of my therapies)—complete healing—came to me that night. I had absolutely no neck pain
then, and have not had one since. I was healed that night.
A million dollars could not have purchased my healing.
God, and God alone, has the power.*

*The memorial of my healing experience for me is my
retaining the cervical pillow. Oh, I don't travel with it any
more. No need to. But, I sleep on this same pillow every
night as a reminder of how God healed me though the
prayer of one of His children.*

*I don't know what God wanted you to learn from me
sharing this up-close, personal, and intimate story today,*

but I hope you have been blessed. As I look back on this experience, I recognize some important things:

__First__, and foremost, I know that God loves me and that He is too wise to make mistakes.

__Second__, I have learned to trust Him and obey His directions even when I don't understand why.

__Third__, I know that God places people in our way (oppressors), who we may feel are despicable, in order that His light may shine through us to them.

And, __fourth__, I know that when we call upon God for healing, He hears, and He answers.

I don't know what your particular dilemma may be today. Perhaps it is of such that only God knows your plight. But I encourage you to listen to His still small voice.

He may be speaking to you and you are ignoring His voice because you just can't believe what He is telling you to do. It just doesn't seem to make sense. But, I encourage you to trust and obey. "Trust and obey; for there is no other way, to be happy in Jesus, but to trust and obey."

God has taken me one step at a time—as a dumb and totally dependent lost sheep. All that I know and all that I am is because He is my Good Shepherd.

This radio program was first aired May 29, 2004, on KCBR-AM 1040 Monument/Colorado Springs. It was worth repeating so others may know about my friend Juanita's unselfish love.

Through Juanita's love, I became a radio host with Crawford Broadcasting and spent five wonderful years broadcasting the *Fragrance of God's Love* radio program in Monument/Colorado Springs and, eventually, WGOD-FM in St. Thomas, Virgin Islands, which was simulcast from their island to St. John, Tortola, and St. Croix.

Chapter 10

MR. IVORY BALL

In Colorado Springs I have been blessed with the three Ts: Trials, Trouble, and Turmoil. However, with these have come the three Js: Jesus, Joy, and Justice. These gifts are often blended, and in my case "joy" came when I met **Ivory Ball**.

When I first arrived in Colorado Springs, I asked God for a *spiritual male* friend. Since I was now living in the Spirit and not in the flesh, I needed someone accepting of my position who would know that it would be a powerless attempt to shake me from my position of celibacy and purity. I was very specific in my request as God and I both knew I had no interest in a boyfriend or a husband, and I certainly had enough girlfriends. I wanted to be able to converse with a single male friend who would...

- **F**ind me good company,
- **R**emember who and Whose we are,
- **I**nterest me in healthful living,
- **E**ngage in wholesome activity,
- **N**ever let physical intimacy be an ingredient for friendship, and
- **D**evote useful and intellectual time to building a lifelong association

I was looking for an extraordinary person: accepting, understanding, and devoted.

Even though I desired to have an unmarried male friend, I did not yearn for a man in my life who would occupy more time than I could afford to give. Every day there were personal goals to accomplish and numerous projects with our ministry that needed my attention.

Eighteen months went by without an answer. It seemed God would never answer this prayer. Finally, I grew satisfied not to have this person in my life, because I felt it was not the will of God. I became content and continued to live life to its fullest.

In Colorado Springs physical fitness, for the first time in my life, became a joyful essential. I had been given a membership to Bally's by my son for my first birthday since moving to the area. I remember when I first started working out: I walked the treadmill for only ten minutes and was tired. Eugene was amazed at my low tolerance, but eventually, and with consistency, I was acclimated to the routine. I exercised at the club four days per week, and my physical fitness and health began improving. (My primary care physician and I were both very happy.)

One morning while getting dressed for Bally's, I prayed another prayer. I asked God to allow me to meet someone, today, with whom I could share the good news about Him and testify of what a good God He had been to me. It was on that day, Friday, September 15, 2000, that into my life walked this *spiritual* friend—Ivory Ball. (When he first told me his name, I wanted to ask if he was ever tempted to change it, but I didn't.)

Ivory is a playwright and a poet, and I am an author and a poet. He is an electrical engineer, and I am mathematically challenged. At the time we met, Ivory was recuperating from the effects of a recent divorce, and I had just been healed from mine. Ivory stated that he was not looking for an intimate relationship with anyone at that time, and since I was not either, the possibility of a friendship was great. (Later he told me that when I mentioned I was a chaplain, it made him feel very comfortable.)

Outside the gym that morning, as Ivory was walking me to my car, he said, "Take a number!" I had no idea what that meant. He saw the puzzled look on my face and then added, "If you have a pen and paper, I will give you my home telephone number." OK, sure! *This is wonderful*, I thought. Here is a stranger who instead of asking for my number gave me his. I was very impressed!

I was, and still am, fascinated with Ivory's tact and understanding of the female mind. He is one of the few men I have met who has never said anything offensive to me or responded in a negative way to anything I say or do. He is able to come back with a positive response even if something is said that may warrant a negative comment. And, when he is with me, he makes me feel like the most important person in the world. I was especially amazed when one evening, while in his home, his best friend (his ex-wife) called and he said to her, "May I call you back? I am entertaining right now." Of course, she said yes, but I was impressed with his dual consideration of both our privacies. What I love most about Ivory is his ability to put any occurrence or imaginary thought into poetic form, and he admires that about me as well. Most of the feelings Ivory and I shared for each other during the time we were exclusive were put into poetry.

Ivory and I saw each other once every other weekend. We attended plays, took long walks, or spent time in our homes: talking, reading our poetry, or discussing differences between our religions—he had studied with the Jehovah's Witness. We had wonderful times together. When we were not together, we talked on the telephone at convenient, and sometimes inopportune, times, and we e-mailed each other almost every day. He even went to church with me once, and that was a "no-no" and a miracle! We often chuckle about that.

Early in our relationship, Ivory mentioned that he was in a state of numbness when it came to being physical with a woman due to his divorce, but he cautioned that in later months he would again feel like being with someone with whom he would eventually want to be intimate. Then he added, "When I find that someone, Marcia, you will be the first to know." I listened, I understood, and I laughed. (No falling in love here was his point; mine was that it would never happen!) From time to time, Ivory would remind me of his future quest, and I would assure him I could handle it.

However, each time we discussed the possibility of him finding a girlfriend, I hoped this would never happen—at least, *"Not now, Lord. Don't let him find anyone else right now, because I am having so much fun!"* However, while I was content and happy with a celibate, "rocking-chair" relationship, Ivory was not.

About six months into our friendship, Ivory called one evening and asked if he could come over for a short visit. I thought it strange, since this was not our scheduled weekend to meet, but I was always excited to see him and was glad to have him visit if only for a little while—he had to be at work early the next morning, and I was on-call at the hospital the next day. When Ivory arrived at my apartment, I was thrilled to see him. He did not seem like his usual self, but he eventually became engrossed in my excitement and glee. I had done most of the talking—as usual. When he said good-bye after our brief time together, I still had not realized that my friend had come to deliver a message that might not have been conducive to my gleeful spirit.

When Ivory reached home, he telephoned. He explained that he had come over to tell me something, and he was unable to say it because of my excitement and expressed happiness. Ivory said, "Marcia, I've found someone..." These three words hit me like a ton of bricks. While my mind said, *"Be happy for him,"* my heart responded differently. It was then that I realized I not only loved this man but I had fallen in love with my friend. The thought of having to pay the respect to this "significant other," that I would have wanted for myself, suddenly took prominence—no more leisure time spent with Ivory, no more indiscriminate phone calls, no more going out together. Ivory now had a girlfriend! Oh, the twinge of a heartbreak.

I don't remember responding to Ivory after he informed me of this new person that would be occupying his life. There was dead silence on my end of the telephone. However, I do remember what he said to me—after asking if I was still on the line and receiving no answer. Ivory said, "Marcia, I did not mean to hurt you." I then hung up the telephone.

Mr. Ivory Ball

Weeks went by as I tried to deal with my emotions. Ivory did try to contact me, but I would not take his phone calls or answer his e-mails. He insisted that nothing had changed with him, and he was still my friend and hoped I was still his friend. He did not understand why I was taking this so hard, as we had talked about this possibility on several occasions. Well, I did not know either, and I knew I could not blame Ivory for the way I felt, but until I was able to sort this out in my mind, I refused to communicate with him. I tried talking to my girlfriends about how I felt, but they too did not understand. Jean said, "You asked God for a friend; He gave you a friend, and now you want to throw that relationship away. Why?" I understood the logic but could not face the reality.

I now had had enough of my female friends. They didn't understand. So, maybe, if I spoke with a male friend, he would be more understanding. So, I called my longtime friend in California, **Pastor Carlyle B. Skinner**, someone I had known since my Allegheny West days. I told him of my plight and then asked him if he understood how I felt. He said, "Yes!" And, his counsel consisted of the following words:

Pastor Skinner said,

1. Don't back away from feelings God created in you.
2. It is natural to have a relationship with the opposite sex that creates emotional bonding—you have things in common, you enjoy going out together, you respect and admire each other. It is OK.
3. The presence of your emotions validates your humanity.
4. Emotions are what God has wired you with.
5. These are signs of being alive, celebrate it!
6. If you love him, it's alright; if you miss him, it's human.
7. *However, don't throw out the baby with the bath water.*

Pastor Skinner's advice was so consoling that I transcribed his words in my diary.

All the advice I had received from my friends was good, yet not good enough. I realized that something supernatural had to happen to cure me from this possessive, demonic behavior. I turned to God again. I needed once more to enjoy the *Fragrance of His Love*.

Six weeks later, on the night before I was to speak for the worship service at my church, I was delivered. The topic I was addressing the next morning was: "Who is your Boaz?" I realized that night that I had lost connection with my Boaz—Jesus Christ. So I asked God to renew my faith and restore my strength. I prayed, "Lord, please take *this thing* away from me so I can continue my friendship with Ivory. Help me keep my commitment to you, and make me worthy to stand before your people tomorrow. I am so lost and confused!" Then, I had a dream:

The Deliverance

In my dream I saw a picture (an oil painting) of Ivory's face. The portrait was carefully framed and hung on my bedroom wall. As I looked at his face, I observed a tear which fell from his left eye.

That was it! I had my answer! God, in that one vision, confirmed that he (Ivory) truly did not mean to hurt me, and that He (God) cared about every aspect of my life and understood exactly how I felt and what I needed. I was delivered at that moment.

When I awoke from my dream, the Holy Spirit brought to my mind how everything I had asked for in a single male friend God had given me, and now I was rejecting that gift. *"You asked me for a 'friend,' and that is just who he has been, who he is, and who he will always be to you."* That day, God removed the attitude of possessiveness from me; I was able to speak for Him; and I was at liberty to maintain the gift of friendship that God had given me in this wonderful human being.

At the end of that day, I was able to e-mail Ivory and ask him to call me at his convenience. When we did speak, I could sense his relief as I told him briefly how God had helped me through this crucial emotional time of my life. Ivory was delighted. I have since had no problems with other women (or men) in Ivory's life. He and I have been friends now for almost a decade. Neither of us has had any regrets, offered any explanations, or made any apologies for our relationship, because we know God has put this pure, undaunted vehicle of friendship in motion. We have different professions, separate religious beliefs, and asymmetrical levels of growth, but there remains a lasting mutual love and respect for one another and a common literary interest in short stories and poetry.

There are other women who have experienced different dimensions of Ivory's love and affection, and many have experienced relationships with him that I will never have. What I do know is that I would not trade the experiences we have journeyed through for any other level of compatibility. I realize too that our journey has been our blessing.

When I asked Ivory to be a member of the board of directors for our nonprofit corporation, CompNar Unlimited, Inc., his only question was, "What would I need to do?" We are thrilled to have Mr. Ball as an important part of our innovative ministry, and I wish him much success in all he does. My prayer is that Ivory will never change in the way he has been taught to treat women and relate to humanity—the children of Jehovah.

Through the love of my friend Ivory Ball, I have learned that true friendships are not made valid by illicit physical intimacy but according to the will of God. And, I understand that many friendships have been ruined by marriage, selfishness, and lust—when taken beyond the boundaries of God's intent.

Chapter 11

THE CHAPLAINCY

Friends who knew me in my early years were familiar with my reluctance to do any type of hospital visitation. Now, they marvel at the fact that I am a hospital chaplain. Some have asked, "Marcia, how did you become a chaplain?" That's a good question, and one I will answer in this chapter. I will also share some wonderful experiences that have happened to me while serving in this position.

One day in 2000 as I sat in Sabbath School at my church, I was so bored. Can you imagine being bored in church? Well I was. I was bored to death. Was it because this particular program was not interesting? You might say so, but that was just partially true. I realized as I sat there that I had been listening to words of truth about the gospel of Christ year after year after year, and I was not continuously sharing with others. On this particular day, I was overly dissatisfied with my Christian outreach experience and wanted to do more to help others.

So, around 10:40 a.m., I left church, got into my car, and started driving around Colorado Springs, asking God to show me where to go and what to do. He led me directly to a local hospital. I started on the upper floor of the hospital, checking with the charge nurse for permission to visit any patient who had not had any visitors or who had no local family members. Permission was granted on the first three floors I visited. I was in high spirits as patients welcomed me into their rooms to share some words from Scripture and pray with them.

When I arrived on the third floor of the hospital, one nurse refused to let me visit any patients. She stated that I could not visit any of her patients without an ID. Oh, no problem! I reached into my purse and pulled out my Colorado driver's license. The nurse looked at my license and said, "Ma'am, you need a hospital ID." When I asked "Why?" she stated that the hospital was on high alert because of a recent homicide on the premises. She added that no one could just walk off the street to visit patients they did not know. "You must be authorized," she added. While I now understood the reason for her objection and was aware that Memorial Hospital was currently a high-profile facility, I was still a bit angry. I left the hospital thinking that of all the nurses, this African-American nurse, this *sister*, was the meanest, as the other nurses had been so kind!

As I stewed over the "rejection" that evening, God showed me that this nurse had done me a wonderful favor. I thought about this and realized that if one of the patients I had visited had suddenly expired after I left the room, I might have been considered a suspect in his or her death. I immediately said a prayer and thanked God for this revelation, and I asked Him to show me a way to penetrate this barrier. Almost immediately, the thought came to call the hospital on Monday morning and see what the requirements were for becoming a volunteer chaplain. I did. I pursued fulfillment of their chaplain's course and became a volunteer.

The journey has been remarkable and has allowed my entrance into a world that I did not know would be so fascinating. I have been able to minister to patients and families because of my life experiences. The educational training I received through the hospital's chaplaincy studies, the support of the medical staff, and the stories of the numerous patients to whom God has allowed me to meet have all contributed to and blessed my ministry.

When it came time for me to officially begin my chaplain's duties, I asked the chief chaplain to allow me to work on the Oncology Unit. This was discouraged, as I was told I had to serve at least six months before such an assignment could be granted. I assured the chaplain that I could handle the work and insisted that this was the only unit that currently appealed to me. Finally, I was allowed to be shadowed, and after two room visits, I was let go to minister to terminally ill patients on my own. What a wonderful journey these past seven years have been—as a unit chaplain and later as an on-call chaplain. I have chosen to share some stories in this book, which may not be verbatim, but are very close.

The first story - One day while doing weekly rounds on the Oncology Unit the charge nurse informed me of a patient whose family was very traumatized by her sudden illness and pending demise. The nurse wanted me to speak to the patient's older son who had not left the hospital or his mother's side since her admission—the nurses and doctors could not get him to go home. The nurse asked if there was anything I could do. "I will try" was my response. This was a first for me, and so I quickly sought help from the Great Psychologist, my Lord and Savior. Within seconds, God gave me the answer of what to say. After entering the room and offering a greeting, I asked the dad if we could go outside and talk for a while. After our brief conversation, I then approached the son and asked the same. Outside the room, I asked the young man three questions, and he answered: *(1) What do you think Mom would want you to be doing right now if she could speak? "She would say I shouldn't be skipping school." (2) What do you believe her ultimate goal is for you? "She wants me to finish high school and go to college." (3) How do you think she would want you to behave right now? "She would want me to be strong for my dad and siblings and just to keep on keeping on."* I prayed with him and then with the entire family. The visit ended with my promise to come back again. On the next occasion of my visit to the unit, the charge nurse stated that she did not know what happened, but the patient's son went home after my visit, and now his visits are intermittent. My thought was *God happened!* When the patient passed away, the dad asked me to perform the eulogy. What a touching and remarkable experience!

The second story - One of my most memorable experiences was being a chaplain to a terminally ill minister and his family. I remember the day when all his children had finally arrived in town. I had the privilege of meeting all seven of them and his beautiful wife. One Sabbath afternoon as

I sat in his room, he asked if I could delay my visit. I told him "Yes." At a point when all the family, including his wife, were absent from the room, he began to speak. He said, "I am happier now than I have ever been!" I thought he would have added that seeing all his children again and reflecting on this beautiful family was the joy of his life, but he did not say that. Instead, he said that he had been reflecting on his life and on how God had used him in service to mankind. He commented that he knew that Jesus had led him all the way. He continued, "When I think back, there is absolutely nothing I would have wanted changed in my life. I am so happy with God!" I had the privilege of attending his funeral service and sharing his parting words to me with his widow—and with her alone. She was ever so thankful that I had shared with her.

The third story - During one of my weekly visits with a female patient, when I offered to pray for her, she asked if she could pray for me. I don't know if she detected that I needed special prayer that day, but I believe God must have chosen her to intercede for me. The patient prayed for those petitions that were in my heart that only God could have known, and she verbalized the requests in words that I could not have chosen. When I left the room, in which I had gone to bless a stranger, I was blessed from the lips of one who God, obviously, used to encourage me.

The fourth story - On one of my on-call days, I was called to the room of a deceased patient, where the husband had refused to let the wife's dead body be removed because of some psychological, personal issues. After entering the room and developing a rapport, I asked the widower why he was hesitant to release his wife's body. He stated that his brother had recently passed away—he had committed suicide under the influence of a controlled substance, and everyone said that he was in hell and will never go to heaven. Then he asked, "What do you say, chaplain?" I had no prepared answer of my own, so I immediately prayed to God. In a matter of one second, God gave me the answer. He said: *Tell this man that I do not judge the action, I judge the motive, and that he will never know if his brother will*

88

be in heaven unless he plans to be there himself. When I verbalized this message to the widower, he thanked me for the answer and wondered why no one had been able to tell him something like this before. I could not respond, but in my heart I thought, *because they had not experienced the fragrance of God's love.* The man immediately released his wife's body, and all was well with the family and the hospital's medical team.

The fifth story - This story has to do with "the power" in a badge. It was Saturday, June 5, 2004. The city of Colorado Springs was having a parade and celebration for the first set of troops that had returned from deployment in Iraq, and many of the main streets in town were blocked off from civilian travel. I had been asked to present the eulogy for a local attorney who had succumbed to breast cancer. It was my privilege to have worked with her in the judicial system, ministered to her and her family while at Memorial Hospital, and followed her to hospice. When her husband asked me if I would do the honors, I was extremely flattered, and I wanted to do my best for them. So, being confronted by barricades on the day of this very important funeral was quite a dilemma. I knew I had to meet with the funeral director at least thirty minutes before the scheduled service, so I left the north area of town and drove into the city as far as I could freely go. All the streets to the funeral home were blocked. Suddenly, the Holy Spirit instructed me to find an officer, show him my chaplain's badge, and inform him of the duties that were awaiting me. I did this, and immediately, road blocks were removed so that I could travel directly to the parking area of the funeral home. As I arrived at my destination, I marveled over "the power" that I thought was in my chaplain's badge, while knowing that God works out the affairs of men not through a badge (or other men) but through the power of His will.

The last story - I know there are no awards for genuine Godly service, but every now and then, God allows us to take a peek at the "rewards" He has for us because of our obedience. He did this for me during one of my on-call visits. It was a Sunday morning, and I had been called by the hospital to minister to the family of a young woman who had experienced irreversible loss of neurological function—she was brain dead—and the family members did not want to let her go. On my drive to the hospital, I asked God what He wanted me to say, or not to say, to this family. In the hospital room, as I spoke, I knew God had placed words in my mouth to utter in this very delicate and crucial situation.

After praying, anointing, and offering words of encouragement, I said good-bye to the family. I proceeded toward the elevator but remembered that I had left my cell phone in the patient's room. On my way back to retrieve the telephone, I passed the nurses' station. As I walked by, I heard the patient's husband say to the charge nurse, "You can remove my wife from life support, as the chaplain has come, and we have been assured that everything is going to be OK." God allowed me to overhear something that reaffirmed my purpose and confirmed His pleasure in my work.

Being a chaplain has been an awesome and rewarding experience. I am confident that there will be a reunion in heaven of the many hundreds of patients and family members whose lives have touched mine and whose lives I have touched. To know that my prayer was the last that a living person heard—and actually one that may have been used to usher them into the kingdom of God—is my earthly heartfelt reward, and God one day will say, "Well done!"

Chapter 12

MY SON JONATHAN

Jonathan passed away on July 12, 2005. He was 29 years old. During the last year of Jon's life, I received his permission to share his story to whomever, whenever, and wherever I pleased. I cannot truly do justice to Jon's story; however, I will try to share with you the son I knew, the wonderful gift of his life, and how God used him to bless me.

We adopted Jonathan when he was 22 months old. As a result of a birth defect and a flawed corrective surgical procedure when he was six months old, our son lost effective use of his bladder and later developed renal failure. Coupled with his physical impairments, Jon exhibited some inappropriate emotional behaviors which we, as parents, thought was a result of his defensive reactions to his medical problems and the teasing he received from classmates. We had dealt with Jon's medical conditions the best we could as parents, and we had taken him to psychologists because of what we felt were abnormal behaviors. However, we always left the psychologists' offices upset, as we were told that there was absolutely nothing wrong with our son, and that we, the parents, needed to learn how to cope with Jon's behaviors.

One day while commuting from work, I listened to a radio program where a therapist talked about symptoms of Attention-Deficit/Hyperactivity Disorder (ADHD). He presented ten recognizable factors pertaining to this diagnosis, and I was able to identify seven of these traits in our son. I was excited that there was a label for what we were experiencing, and I rushed home and told my husband all about my new discovery. We were both relieved that there was a diagnosis for what we had been describing as blatant disobedience and an explanation as to why others had labeled our son as "bad." We now understood that Jon's inability to focus, his over activity, and his impulsive behaviors were symptoms of ADHD.

Even though for a period I was a stay-at-home mom, Jon was his dad's son. I had very little to do with Jon's upbringing, as Gene assumed primary custodial responsibilities for all activities pertaining to Jon's social interaction, school enrollment, and medical supervision. Understandably, and naturally, Jon (as did his brother) took his father's death very hard. I remember after Gene died, Jon said to me, "Mommy, who is going to tell me what to do now?" I looked into the eyes of my now seventeen-year-old son and had no answers for him.

Jon and I both knew that I alone, even though I tried, could not handle all of the medical, social, and economic concerns and still maintain full-time employment to ensure income and health insurance for me and both the children. It was at this juncture that I learned about the U.S. Social Security Administration and benefits available for disabled individuals like my son: SSI, Medicaid, etc. (Our family had been so self-sufficient all our life that these outside resources were a new phenomenon.) I thought *Why not apply for some help from the government?* So, I did! But, even with this extra financial and medical help for Jon, his behavior and his street life made it impossible for us to live together without me losing my villa. I had to find a behavioral center or a home for special needs children where Jon could live and use his government benefits to pay for his care.

We did find a place (several places). However, Jon refused to be compliant in any environment. When I would visit and ask what was it about these places that bothered him, he would say, "Besides the fact that this place is not home, I cannot stand curfews and obeying rules." I mentioned to him that at home there were curfews and rules as well, and since he could not abide by them at home, he must at least try to be compliant in his home away from home. But, Jon was not "feeling" this. One day he informed me that he was going to take to the streets, and if he ever got in trouble with the law and the cops told him to stop or they'd shoot, they would just have to shoot him in the back.

While still living in Florida, my son and I became estranged from each other. Jon had taken to the streets as he had promised, and my survival as a widow and mother of two fatherless children was paramount. I was determined that Jon's new lifestyle would not invade our home and take me on a trip to skid row. Thus began our ten-year estrangement.

When I moved to Colorado Springs, and as was prophesied by Ivory Jackson (in an earlier chapter), I was constantly aware that Jon would eventually be moving here to reside with the rest of the family. The *how* and the *when* were unknown to me; but, over the years, God worked it out so that Jon lost his love for lawlessness and I was prepared to welcome him home again. Questions I asked myself were: Had he changed? Have I changed? If so, and if not, who would be responsible for our cohesiveness and cohabitation? I knew that only God could intervene and that He would do it through the fragrance of His love for me and my children. This thought humbled me and allowed me to be totally dependent on God for all decisions.

Even though we were apart for many years, Jon and I stayed in touch through letters. In late 2001 and early 2002, his letters were all about him coming to live with family and his prayers that God would grant his petition to see his mother and brother one more time before he died. During that same period, God began to prepare me (as He was preparing Jon) for our reunion. God began to work in my heart through different sermons I would hear and different Bible texts I would read. For example, one evening while coming home from work, I was listening to KCBR/AM, and there was a preacher saying, "If you still remember, you have not forgiven." Then, one morning I read Isaiah 58:6-7 [KJV] for my devotional thought:

Is not this the fast that I have chosen? to loose the bands of wickedness, to undo the heavy burdens, and to let the oppressed go free, and that ye break every yoke? Is it not to deal thy bread to the hungry, and that thou bring the poor that are cast out to thy house? when thou seest the naked, that thou cover him; and that thou hide not thyself from thine own flesh?

Wow! What condemnation! I realized I still remembered some of the difficult times Jon and I had in Florida and that I was hiding myself from my own flesh. In a gradual stream of divine intervention, my son and I were reunited at the Colorado Springs Airport on October 5, 2002. He flew in on a red-eye flight two days after major surgery in Orlando. When I saw my son again, after so many years, I knew, beyond the shadow of a doubt, that he had changed. Even though Jon deplaned in a wheelchair and was very sick, his attitude was different. When I asked him how his flight had been, he said, "Mom, I felt as though I was being carried on angels' wings!" He was glad to see me, and I was so delighted to be making a fresh start with my son.

During the first year we were together again, something quite miraculous happened. I was on my way to the recording studio to do our weekly radio program. As I was driving to the station, I heard a song on my car radio that I had never heard before. It was by Denise LaSalle, and it was called "If I'm Only for Myself." When I heard that song, it convicted me to do the *Fragrance of God's Love* radio broadcast about my son and our ten years of estrangement. I had never talked about my family life on radio before; and certainly had not planned to do that—ever—but I knew God was directing me to do just that. When I arrived at the studio, I asked our producer, John Michaels, if he had ever heard this Denise LaSalle song and whether or not he had it in the computer. Yes! John had the song, which I asked him to play as the prelude to (and also at the end of) the program. I had never done a radio program without notes. On radio I am always fully scripted. Messages are prepared at home under the influence of the Holy Spirit and always nicely typed up for reading. However, today, as I sat in front of the microphone, it was evident that I would be speaking (without notes) about my relationship with my son and under the direction of the Holy Spirit.

Before delivering the message, I did a brief introduction, and then we played the song by Ms. LaSalle. When I began to speak, I knew it would not take a keen listener to know that I had been sobbing and that the message was from the very heart of God. After talking about the years my son and I were apart, how God had reunited us, and the wonderful time I was now having with my son, I prayed for all the parents and children who could relate to this story. I made a desperate appeal to those who had not sought reconciliation with family members to do so. As I prayed for our listeners, I saw and felt shackles falling from individuals who had turned against family members or family members against them. At the end of the program, I felt I had operated completely out of my comfort zone (speaking for 28 minutes without notes), and I sought validation from God. I sent up a silent prayer, asking Him to show me a sign that I had indeed done what He wanted me to do. I told Him, "If this program was fully Yours then allow just one person to call us immediately after the program airs."

The recording was done on a Thursday, and the half-hour program aired at 11:00 a.m. on Saturday. The next morning when I checked our corporate voice mail, someone had called at 11:31 a.m. the day before in response to the broadcast she had just heard. When I returned the listener's call that day, this grandmother stated that she had been estranged from her children and her grandchildren for many years, and when she heard the broadcast through my tears and the prayer that was prayed, she was delivered. When I hung up the telephone, after our conversation and prayer, I thanked God for what He had done!

Jon listened to that program a few weeks later, and he was very pleased. He also consented to be a guest on another radio program, and listening to that recording truly touched my heart as I heard my son talk to the interviewer about his upbringing, his contrary lifestyle after his dad died, and the reunion he was now having with family members.

During the last two and a half years that we spent with Jon in Colorado Springs, I witnessed a heightened level of maturity with which my son had been blessed and knew that what he had learned in life was beyond any parental influence. Not only had Jon matured during the years we were apart, but he was more street-smart than ever. In addition, he was wise in the way he addressed and responded to individuals, especially those who may not have been too kind to him. He had mellowed a great deal, and his attitude was: "Mom, it is what it is." The last thirty months of my son's life were the happiest and most fulfilling time of our lives together.

In Colorado Springs, God had made provisions for us—even before Jon arrived—of which we were totally unaware. Our heavenly Father had people (doctors, other medical personnel, church family, etc.), places, and services available to us that we did not know we would need or had even looked into prior to this new living arrangement. My son's tenure in Colorado Springs was not without challenges, but it did not disrupt or destroy my way of living or my time in ministry. When my son died, he died in peace and with the knowledge of how much he had been loved.

We are very grateful to "the village" and "the villagers" that helped us raise our son Jonathan. If I would attempt to name everyone who had been a part of his life, I am sure someone would be overlooked; however, each individual knows who he/she is, and his/her reward is in heaven.

We realized that Jon could have departed this life while in Florida (or I could have done the same while in Colorado), and we would not have had a chance to make amends or express our love for each other. But God allowed us an earthly gathering that helped to prepare each of us for the heavenly homecoming.

Through the love of my son Jon, I have learned that it is not a human privilege to give up on individuals, we do not hold a measuring stick for anyone, God provides chances for reconciliation even when we think it is impossible, and when we are about to give up on our circumstance, God has one more move.

Chapter 13

OUR INTERNET MINISTRY

The "Fragrance of God's Love" media broadcast, which includes our local radio and television programs, is now archived on the Internet. For many years, the radio program was the joy of my life. As mentioned in Chapter 9, it was Evangelist Juanita Johnson who introduced me to radio, but I know that she was used by God in helping us to expand the ministry of *The Complete Woman/Man Seminars* via that medium.

Prior to my first attempt at broadcasting in 2000, I had asked God to give me five families in Colorado Springs with whom I could conduct Bible studies. He knew I was not a knock-on-your-door type of person, especially since many homeowners in the neighborhood around my church had dogs that were not afraid to attack. (I had been a victim of a dog bite years before and did not want to repeat the experience.) So, God answered my prayer by giving me, instead, a radio broadcast where numerous Bible studies have reached myriad of unknown individuals (unknown to me that is). The radio program preceded our television program (of the same name), and had a longer duration. Our television program aired concurrently with the radio program but only for a few months.

Numerous individuals have asked how the name of our media broadcast was selected. I usually say the idea came from God through the writings of the Apostle Paul. "Fragrance of God's Love" truly is a depiction of the message recorded in 2 Corinthians 2:14-16 [KJV], which says,

> Now thanks be unto God, which always causeth us to triumph in Christ, and maketh manifest the savour of his knowledge by us in every place.

For we are unto God a sweet savour of Christ, in them
that are saved, and in them that perish:
To the one we are the savour of death unto death;
and to the other the savour of life unto life. And who is
sufficient for these things?

Death to Death: - "Testifying Christians are the smell of
death to those who are perishing, not because the gospel
message has become evil-smelling or death-dealing, but
because in rejecting the life-giving grace of God unbeliev-
ers choose death for themselves" (NIV).

Life to Life: - "To those who welcome the gospel of
God's grace, Christians with their testimony are the fragrance of life" (NIV).

Actually, the Spirit of God gave us both the name and the
song "Sheltered in the Arms of God" by The Gaither Singers
which is the postlude to the radio broadcast. We know that *fragrance* is not the Spirit, but it is the Spirit in us that gives off
the fragrance. "Fragrance of God's Love" has become a global,
household theme in many homes through our streaming Internet
audio and video on: http://www.completeseminars.org. Being
able to study, testify, and impart to others through this medium
has been a great blessing.

When we began our radio program, we had no idea how
we would pay for the airings. But we knew God had a plan,
and by faith, we signed our contract. Shortly after this agreement, and my trying to pay for the program from my already
"insufficient" payroll check, I shared our book, *The Complete Wo/Man: An Index to the Heart*, with my friend **Greta
Bartley-Hamilton**. Greta was, then, living in another state.
After reading the book, she called and asked if I would send
a copy to each of her three sisters. She then asked the cost
of the books, including her own, along with shipping and
handling charges. I reluctantly told her forty-five dollars, as
I was willing to send these books as gifts. Greta stated that
she would have her bank prepare a check and send me the
money as soon as possible.

Upon receipt of the check from Greta's bank, we noticed that the check was for a much larger amount than was warranted. I immediately picked up my cell phone, called Greta, and informed her of the obvious error. Greta began to laugh. When I asked her why she was laughing? She said, "Marcia, the bank did not make a mistake. That is the amount I authorized, and you will be receiving a similar amount every month to pay for your radio program." I was amazed that someone who (at that time) had never heard any of the programs, and was not aware of our financial need, was able to be so generous. For almost four years, our radio program was fostered by the benevolence of this wonderful woman who believed in the ministry and the power of God to reach all people. Greta continues to promote our ministry—and why not? When we incorporated, she became a member of our board of directors.

Others who are, and were, truly instrumental in helping us stay on the airways and on the Internet include **Sandra and Roy Morgan** who have been consistent in their giving to Christian radio. **Bob Bailey**, our CPA, and his wife **Tina** have made sizeable contributions (and Bob offers accounting services at no charge). Our corporate attorney, **Dennis K. Thomas**, also represents us pro-bono. **Attorney Michael Carpenter**, of the law firm of Carpenter and Cassens, and a member of our board of directors, is also an annual contributor to the broadcast.

I will be eternally grateful to individuals such as: **Steve Reiter**, senior recording engineer for Focus on the Family, who dispelled my "fear" of the microphone and instructed me in voice level balancing and also produced our first set of commentary CDs; **John Michaels**, formerly with Crawford Broadcasting, who produced all of the radio programs recorded at the KCBR/AM studios in Colorado Springs; and **Armstead Enterprise**, Eugene Armstead, proprietor, who organized our citywide conferences, directed and produced Conference CDs, produced some radio programs and all of the television programs, and created our Website with its streaming audio and videos. Eugene also selected the beautiful kiosk that serves as the backdrop for the television programs.

Ministry does not pay, or, at least, it has not paid us as yet. It has cost us a lot to have accomplished what we have thus far. It took all the inheritance of my late husband to fund this ministry, and I know that our family has been, are, and will be forever blessed as a result of having used what we were awarded from his death to accomplish this feat.

Through our Internet ministry, we have been able to reach many people who live in places we have not traveled or to which we may never go. Our hope is that this medium will reach hundreds and thousands of individuals in spite of financial limitations, unforeseen circumstances, or unfortunate encounters. We pray that those who have listened, are listening, and have yet to listen to our programs will truly be blessed by "The Fragrance of God's Love" as He has willed it for their lives.

Chapter 14

AN "ANGEL" AT THE VA

There would have been no Internet ministry without the technical skills and pursuit of my son Eugene and the inheritance my younger son Jonathan and I received from the Veterans Administration.

I remember when Eugene had moved away from Colorado Springs, and I went to visit him in January 2002. He shared with me how God had shown him his role in helping to further establish our ministry. Up to this point, *The Complete Woman / Man Seminars* extended just as far as we could travel. During the week, each of our consultants stayed busy in their unique places of employment, and on the weekends, we would take to the transit systems with the message of teaching audiences how to be complete in Jesus Christ. We were also involved with two radio broadcasts—locally on KCBR/AM in Colorado Springs and in Orlando/Kissimmee with Vice-President Jean Anderson hosting a similar "Fragrance of God's Love" broadcast.

Now, Eugene was talking about global outreach, and I did not quite understand that. He talked about streaming audio and video to someone who knew very little about technology. I was used to traveling with placards and weighty handouts; now he spoke of a thumb drive, which was all we needed to carry when doing our presentations. Wow! Whatever all that was sounded exciting, but I could not quite envision the total plan. I knew there were big corporations that utilized this type of technology, but we had not quite reached that level of operation. However, what I did understand was, "Mom, it will take a lot of money to do what I am planning for the ministry, and I know we do not have the capital." This was as clear as a bell, but I assured Eugene that I was still in hopes of winning my appeal against the Veterans Administration (VA) regarding his father's untimely death, and we could use that money for ministry. My son then said, "Mom, you are chasing a pipedream and have been doing so for several years now. I know God can provide, but let's stop dreaming." My response: "Oh, you of little faith."

As it was, Eugene was partially right. It had been eight years that the VA had denied my claim that my late husband's Leukemia was directly associated to Agent Orange, which he was exposed to while on his tour of duty in Vietnam.

I had appealed their denials for eight years on behalf of my children and myself. Now entering the ninth year, I was certain that God was going to hear our cry. I had dreamed about receiving money—a small sum and one large sum—and I knew the larger portion was not for me. Prior to that dream, however, I prayed to the Lord, and I told him that if my husband did not die as a result of the Agent Orange poisoning, then I truly did not want a dime of the government's money, but if he did, I would not rest until my children and I were compensated for his death.

I was open to God's instructions to let me know what to do at this point. So, I listened as He instructed me on how to respond to the organization's eighth denial letter. God said, "No longer talk about yourself or your children. In this final appeal, I want you to talk about me." I obeyed. In my cover letter of 2001 to the VA, I inscribed a paragraph informing them that in spite of their many denials, I was trusting in God that He would allow my sons and I to be compensated for the loss of their father and my husband. I further stated that my late husband's file was not in the hands of the VA, but residing in the hands of the One who, among other miracles, opened blinded eyes, healed crippled people, and parted the Red Sea for the children of Israel to cross over on dry land.

It was one oppressive day in March 2002 when it seemed all hope of getting out of my financial rout was diminishing that I received the usual annual response to my appeal letter from the VA. I was in a hurry when I retrieved the large brown envelope from my post office box, so I simple threw it in the back of my car. As I was driving toward the highway, the Holy Spirit kept urging me to stop and open the package. I did, and immediately flipped through the front pages and directly to page 11 where the

VA's decision was always printed. To my surprise, the words: You have been "denied," were replaced with: You have been "awarded!"

My three years of famine in Colorado Springs had finally ended! I had received retroactive Death Indemnity Compensation (DIC) benefits from the VA in acknowledgement of my late husband having given his life in the service of his country—effective from the date of Gene's death to the day I was remarried. (Four years of benefits were deducted for the time and duration of my remarriage.) My son Jonathan, because of his disabilities, was also eligible for DIC benefits and would be receiving a monthly check from the VA. In the first distribution of funds, I received just enough to pay for the loan on my car, publish our first book, pay all other creditors, rebuild my credit, and become debt free.

I had been informed by the VA in St. Petersburg, Florida, that there was a statute instituted under the administration of former US President Bill Clinton which made provisions for a spouse who had remarried and divorced to be able to resume benefits from the time of the dissolution until the time of the award. This meant that I was due a second lump sum equal to the first that would cover the period from my divorce to the date of the award. However, this was something that I had to pursue after the transfer of my file from Florida to Denver, Colorado. I waited for the transfer of the file and then several months later began to call the Denver office for the process in receiving the balance of my allotment.

After several phone calls to that office, where they acknowledged receiving the file but denied that there were any other provisions for subsequent DIC benefits, I became very frustrated. But, as usual, I knew the Lord would work things out eventually. I was even challenged to find the referenced statute for proof of its existence before the department would entertain any more discussions concerning this matter. Well, since I had been out of my financial *quicksand*, I procrastinated.

When my son Jonathan began residing with me in Colorado Springs, I called the VA on his behalf to initiate distribution of his monthly benefits to our checking account. Well, I experienced another roadblock. I was told that I needed to have guardianship and that I was being transferred to a customer service representative in the Guardianship Department. By then, I was so fed up with the administration that I started to terminate the phone call. However, the Holy Spirit said, *"Don't hang up! Let this call go through."* I was obedient. When the representative answered, I told her what I needed, and she stated that she would pull the physical file, review it, and get back with me. Within two hours, I received a return call from this woman who had taken the time to review the file and give an accurate and informed response. The representative stated that she had reviewed my file and found that there was unfinished business: (1) I was due another award payment, and (2) not only would my son be commencing receipt of his monthly benefits, but he too had retroactive DIC benefits that were due him. Unfortunately, my oldest son was only eligible for VA educational benefits (as were Jon and I). When I received that information from someone who was knowledgeable of the statutes and the process, all I could say was: "Thank you, Lord." Surprisingly, but affirmatively, the representative's response was: "Isn't He a wonderful God?" I had never heard this type of response from a public service representative before or since. That day I knew God had put **"an angel"** in place to arrange this exchange and solve the problems.

It took months for the process to be completed, but I was not stressed or anxious. I knew those monies were not for us, but that the funds were to be used to further the work of God through "The Fragrance of God's Love" media broadcast and Internet ministry. Jon voluntarily donated all his money, with the exception of $2,000, to the ministry, and I added my second allotment to the pot. It was with these funds that we were able to put in place the mechanics needed to do a global outreach that would bless the hearts and minds of men and women who came in contact with our ministry.

Our inheritance is gone, but it has been invested in saving souls. I have learned that even though people who are blessed may not give their financial support to the work that we are engaged in, God has ways and means of keeping us afloat. There are times now when funds are low that I try to remind God of the investment we made to Him and ask if He will continue to bless us as He has blessed us before. The answer always comes in three questions: *(1) Have I not always blessed you and yours with or without money? (2) Do I not continue to bless you daily? and (3) Is there not much more to come?* It is because of these assurances that we press forward—against all odds and among multiple challenges—in the work that God has called us to do.

Chapter 15

JESUS

I am a witness that God can do whatever He desires, with whomever He chooses, to accomplish any task. The only prerequisite for effective servant leadership is full surrender. I realize that everything I have done outside of an un-surrendered life has been tough, tricky, and inconsequential.

I have **read** that the most difficult thing for a Christian to do is surrender, and I have **learned** that one thing a Christian must do to meet God's approval is to surrender. The process of *surrender* is recognizing you are living in sin, desiring to stop sinning, asking forgiveness for the wrong you have done, and accepting the grace of God to keep you from returning to a sinful life.

It took a long time for me to learn and understand that. Not because I was unfamiliar with the process, but because I felt there was time to surrender my life after I had done all there was to do outside of Christ—even though I was miserable. Like many others, my surrender came about because God wanted to spend eternity with me and He had to jiggle my chain. It was under divine pressure that I gave up a hellbound lifestyle and a pretentious facade to accept God's gift of salvation.

I thank God for **Jesus**, who shed his blood that I can be reconciled to the Father. And I thank Him for the Holy Spirit that urged me to give Him my all. In the presence of a holy God, one's heart must be pure and hands must be clean. It is only the blood of Jesus that can ensure that purity.

Often when I am introduced to an audience, I am flattered to hear my host say wonderful things about me and about our ministry. The words of achievements sound good and perhaps are impressive to some, but a true introduction that could precede any type of public speaking is: *"I was sinking deep in sin, far from the peaceful shore; very deeply stained within sinking to rise no more. But the Master of the sea heard my despairing cry, and from the waters lifted me, now safe am I."* I consider myself a sinner saved by grace because God's love lifted me.

It is unfortunate that it has taken many decades of living for me to have surrendered my life fully to God. When I think of all the wasted years of trying to achieve without His power, I feel regretful. However, when I reflect on the past sixteen years in ministry, I rejoice knowing that it is never too late, and that God meets us where we are.

To the reader, let me say that there is no sin that God cannot forgive, no life that He will not restore, and no relationship He will not destroy or put in place to save His children. I know that my life experiences (too numerous for all to have been included in this book) have all served to make me a better person. And, when I read in Revelation 22:13 [KJV], "I am Alpha and Omega, the beginning and the end, the first and the last," I am convinced that nothing is more important than knowing that the God who created me is the God who is in charge of my being, and He is the God to whom I must give an account at the end of the journey.

Through the love of my friend Jesus, I have been saved to serve, and I will live for Him because He has died for me.

ABOUT THE AUTHOR

Marcia Beverly Armstead is author of *The Complete Wo/Man: An Index to the Heart*, which she describes as "an outline to a lifeline." Thousands have been blessed by this inspirational book and through the ministry of *The Complete Woman/Man Seminars*.

Marcia is president and CEO of CompNar Unlimited, Inc., which is the parent company for *The Complete Woman/Man Seminars* and the "Fragrance of God's Love" media broadcast.

Marcia is also a poet and a freelance writer and a contributor to the *Women of Color Study Bible*, a 2000 publication of Nia Publishing, Atlanta, Georgia. She and her seminar consultants have shared the fragrance of God's love on radio, television, and in group seminars throughout the United States, and to the islands of Jamaica, St. Thomas, St. Croix, Tortola, St. John, and Nassau, Bahamas.

Marcia is happily unmarried. She is the mother of one surviving son and the blessed grandmother of three.

We invite you to view the complete
selection of titles we publish at:

www.LNFBooks.com

or write or email us your praises,
reactions, or thoughts about this
or any other book we publish at:

TEACH Services, Inc.

P.O. Box 954

Ringgold, GA 30736

info@TEACHServices.com

CPSIA information can be obtained
at www.ICGtesting.com
Printed in the USA
FSOW04n2033080915
10637FS

9 781572 586093